THE SON

The Foundation

JESSICA ONSAGA

This series is dedicated to the sons of God who will say "YES" to Yahweh no matter the cost. May these books help you grow in sonship and maturity in your walk with Christ.

The Sonship Series: The Foundation
Jessica Onsaga

The Sonship Series: The Foundation
Copyright © 2022

Published by Seraph Creative
ISBN 978-1-958997-39-0

www.seraphcreative.org

TABLE OF CONTENTS

Foreword   6

Introduction   8

Chapter 1: The GOOD News!   11

Chapter 2: Our New Identity   26

Chapter 3: The Process of Transformation   32

Chapter 4: Engaging with Yahweh   42

Chapter 5: Nuts and Bolts of Engaging   51

Chapter 6: Trouble-shooting Getting Stuck   60

Chapter 7: Growing Up   69

Chapter 8: The Mysterious and Wonderful   75

Resources for the Journey Ahead   81

Poems of a Lover of Jesus   83

FOREWORD

The Gospel is the power of God to salvation

In the Christian world there are many ministries, methods and modalities on how to help you mature, be healed and access the promises of salvation. Many of these are excellent ministries, and performed by competent Christians of good heart. However, only the hearing, understanding and believing Gospel has the power to change your being. Only the finished work of Christ can cause and sustain a transformed life.

If any person be in Christ, they are a new creation

More important than the minister or methodology is the understanding of who you are in Christ. Who is being prayed for? Who is being prophesied to? Who is doing 'spiritual warfare'?

Are you a Christian on Earth, looking up to God in Heaven for help? If you believe so, you will need ministries, priests and the 'next move' of God to bring and sustain change to your life. However, if you know you are a new creation - a Son of God, raised and seated in heavenly places, having already received everything you need for life and Godliness - then all ministry is simply helping you realize and release what is already yours - in any area of your life.

Better still, once you realise the answer to your prayer has already been given to you at salvation and sits within, you may not need ministry at all. Instead, you will live in the reality of your new creation from your relationship directly with God Himself!

(If we stop asking God to do what He has done already and stop asking Him to do what he has asked us to do - most of our prayer life would be over).

They who have entered Christ's rest have ceased from their strivings and works

The transformation of a person's life to be more like Christ is a rest. A rest in that it was Jesus' idea, Jesus' finished payment and Jesus' continual work in you that changes you - spirit, soul and body. How much fasting, how much bible memorization, how many prayer meetings would you need to do to become like Christ?! It is impossible for us, and thus, it is an amazing gift. A gift of the person of Jesus Christ living inside you.

This series of books is here to awaken you to the amazing reality of what you have already received. As you read, the Holy Spirit will do the work to help you see, believe and live in all that He has promised (and thus, is already yours - already you!)

Remember, it is God who causes you to will and to act according to His good purpose. Our only role is to say, "Yes Lord. Be it unto me according to your word."

From Glory to Glory
Chris Blackeby

INTRODUCTION

Welcome to The Sonship Series! It is my joy and honor to be on this journey of discovering more of God with you. Whether you have been raised in church or if you just found out about Jesus, there is infinitely more that we can learn and discover about God. This series of books was written for those who are hungry for more and are willing to go beyond their boxes and ideas. Most people can agree that God is way bigger than our pea-brains...but for some reason, many people are unwilling to look beyond the comfortable box of their theology. If you lean into what these books discuss, this series will take you on an adventure exploring God and learning how to grow in your relationship and identity in Him. I am passionate about helping the body of Christ fall in love with Jesus and walk in sonship, and these books will do that if you let them! If God can speak through a donkey...I'm sure He can speak to you in this series.

Throughout these books, I aim to break down simple but powerful concepts so that we can grow more in our walk with Jesus. This first book, The Foundation, is the theological foundation for the rest of the series and explains the nuts and bolts of how to have a two-way friendship with God. It is necessary to read this book first so you are ready to receive what the rest of the series covers. Book 2, Growing in Sonship, explores how to be a son of God on the earth and mature in our relationship with Yahweh. Book 3, BEcoming Whole, is a workbook-styled book that addresses our soul wounds (which block us from walking in what God has for us). And finally, Book 4, Cultivating Authority, discusses walking in the power and authority God gave us through intimacy and relationship with Him. *I do want to mention that it would be good for Books 1-3 to be read before reading the fourth and final book (Cultivating Authority). If you skip ahead to the "fun stuff" in book 4, you will not have the necessary foundation to receive and walk in the "fun stuff" I discuss.*

Everything I write in these books is intended to help you start a conversation with Yahweh and go deeper in Him. I won't quote every verse or fully explain every topic I write about. That is intentional and by design. If I fully explain everything, most people will be satisfied just to have more head knowledge instead of bringing the information to Jesus. To prevent that from happening, my goal in these books is to give you just a taste, an appetizer just enough to make you hungry, so that you go to Jesus with these things. JESUS is our source. HE is the healer, and it is HIS truth that transforms our soul. The words in this series will only become more head knowledge if you do not allow JESUS to show you the heart revelation in them. (I define head knowledge as anything you have learned about Jesus but don't truly know or believe in your heart/soul.) Head knowledge doesn't touch the deep feelings and beliefs of the soul. We were never created to live from knowledge. We were created to live in RELATIONSHIP with all of the Godhead. And through relationship with them, we renew our minds and transform our lives. That is the singular most important thing for any believer—learning to abide in and live from our oneness with God. So, when I am explaining things in this series, I am hoping to give you just enough information for you to go to Jesus and ask Him about it. Jesus can then sift what I am saying and explain how it applies to you in your special circumstances.

The topics in this book and series are from my walk with Jesus. The things I share have been learned through great pain and trials— or they came from my quiet time with God. As I write this series, most of the time I will cut right to the meat and be as brief and direct as possible. Personally, I do not care for lots of fluff, and I like to get right to the point when teaching, so naturally, that is how these books will be. They are intense and nutrient-packed, so they need time to be digested slowly. You will get the most out of these books by reading them multiple times and by stopping to talk to Jesus every time something sticks out to you. Let HIM speak to you, these books are just a springboard to talking with Him about the topics covered.

I believe there are gravely intense times ahead, and that is also why I am writing this series. I don't want you to be deceived or dismayed when life gets hard. I hope these books help you stand firm in Truth during dark times. In spite of what's to come, I am confident there will be the greatest outpouring of God's Spirit on the earth. These truly are the most exciting times to be alive! All of Heaven is watching eagerly for this transition to unfold. There is nothing to fear. This is the age of the revealing of Jesus Christ. So, I invite you to lean into Jesus with all you have. Give Him your undying, unwavering YES! The best is yet to come!

Chapter One:

THE GOOD NEWS!

The gospel. It's actually REALLY good news! It is also the cornerstone of the foundation for the Sonship Series. The story of the gospel is what everything else builds upon. What we believe about the gospel, God, and who we are affects every aspect of life. So, this is where we must start.

I was born into religion, and I knew how to play its game well. Even as a child, I always loved God, but I was stuck in a very distant, obeying my loving master, type relationship with Him. When I was 16, my religious world turned upside down at a winter camp. I encountered Jesus for the first time in a personal way. My old paradigm of religion was blown up, and I began my eternal journey of discovering the majesty of Yahweh and my oneness with Him. I can now see that religion taught me a distorted and perverted gospel, so let's clear something up.

This is how I would *roughly* summarize "the gospel" that religion taught me:

I was told that there is an all-powerful, creator God and that He is very good, holy, and just. He made everything and gave Adam and Eve one simple rule. They broke the simple rule, and all of humanity was doomed and damned because of the original two people who disobeyed. Because of God's holiness, He couldn't be around sin. Worse yet, people needed to be punished for their sins through eternal damnation. But God loves us so much that He sent His only Son, Jesus, to die for our sins so we could be saved from God's wrath and punishment. Jesus came as a sacrificial lamb to take the wrath and punishment due to us. He came to earth as a baby, lived, and was killed. Then Jesus was raised three days later from the dead, victorious over sin! If you believed in Jesus, then you could be saved from hell. But that salvation from sin didn't really start until you died because you would always be stuck in sin during your time here on earth. Religion teaches that we are supposed to try our best not to sin and be "good Christians" while on earth till we finally die and get to go to Heaven...or that we need to try our best not to sin and be "good Christians" until Jesus comes back, whichever happened first.

I believed this gospel. I taught this gospel. I went door to door doing evangelism with this gospel. And I was wrong...so very wrong. It took years of undoing for Jesus to get through and show me how wrong I was. And I am going to assume that you were probably taught a similar gospel and had the same feelings. So first, I will dissect some of religion's gospel and prove why it is wrong. Then, I will share the gospel according to the scriptures. I pray that you continue to dissect what you were taught and test it against the Bible to see how it holds up.

Myth 1:

God's holiness can't be around sin.

WRONG! God CAN be around sin. GOD came to be with Adam in the garden after he sinned, and ADAM was the one who hid. Over and over again in the scriptures, GOD comes down to be with sinful people even before Jesus came to deal with sin. The only verse I can find supporting this myth is:

> Habakkuk 1:13 (Amp.) "Your eyes are too pure to approve evil, And You cannot look favorably on wickedness. _Why then do You look favorably on those who act treacherously?_" [Emphasis mine]

Even at the end of the verse, Habakkuk admits that God looks upon sin. God IS holy, just, and good. All this is true! It's just different than how I was taught. And His holiness doesn't keep Him from us. God promises never to leave us or forsake us. That's a promise that is given multiple times in different books of the Bible.

And let's talk about what sin is. There's much debate over sin in religious circles. We know from the Bible that sin is an archery term for missing the mark. And we know that the wages of sin is death. But what does that mean? I would define sin as ANY separation from Yahweh. He is LIFE itself, so any separation from life would equal death. That's why Jesus said it is a sin to have murder in our hearts even if we haven't acted on it. The murderous thoughts that we allow show that part of our heart is separated from Life Himself. It shows that part of our heart is yielded to a lie and that agreement causes death to us. The murder in our heart is sin because it causes separation from Yahweh. So, God CAN be around us and our sin, but WE are the ones who hide from God because His light exposes our separation and pain.

Myth 2:

Because God is just, we have to be punished for our sins. Jesus came down to take our punishment and appease God's wrath.

WRONG! There are SO many twisted things about this. God's wrath is possibly the most misunderstood attribute of God. There are no verses that I have been able to find supporting the idea that God poured His wrath on Jesus. There are verses about God laying the sins of the world on Jesus, but that is very different from God's wrath being poured out. IF this statement were true, then GOD changed at the event of the cross. He was full of wrath, and now He's supposedly been appeased because of the cross. (At least until the end times, then He's wrathful again.)

Hebrews 13:8 (BSB) "Jesus Christ is the same yesterday and today and forever."

Hebrews 1:3 (TPT) "The Son is the dazzling radiance of God's splendor, the exact expression of God's true nature-His mirror image"!

Note: If God changed at the cross, then He is not the same yesterday, today, and forever.

And let's talk about this punishment idea. Punishment doesn't help us or bring transformation. It says in the word that Jesus came for the blind, the sick, and the lost. Punishment can never make a blind person see or a sick person well. We needed a total transformation and a savior, NOT punishment.

Luke 19:10 (BSB) "For the Son of Man came to seek and to save the lost."

John 3:17 (BSB) "For God did not send His Son into the world to condemn the world, but to save the world through him." [Emphasis mine]

2 Corinthians 5:19 (Amp.) "that is, that God was in Christ reconciling the world to Himself, not counting people's sin against them [but canceling them]."

Myth 3:

If you believe Jesus died and rose again, then you can be saved from hell. Here on earth though, you will always be stuck in sin till you die.

WRONG! How powerless is Jesus if He can only save us from sin AFTER we die? There are no verses supporting the idea that we will be stuck in sin (sinners) until death. If this were true, then DEATH would be liberating us from a sin-filled world into the arms of Jesus! Jesus isn't waiting for us to die so we can live an abundant life only in Heaven. Instead, the New Testament is FULL of verses discussing our transformation into a new creation.

> 2 Corinthians 5:17 (Amp.) "Therefore if anyone is in Christ [that is, grafted in, joined to Him by faith in Him as Savior], he is a new creature [reborn and renewed by the Holy Spirit]; the old things [the previous moral and spiritual condition] have passed away. Behold, new things have come [because spiritual awakening brings a new life]."

> Colossians 1:13 (Amp.) "For He has rescued us and has drawn us to Himself from the dominion of darkness, and has transferred us to the kingdom of His beloved Son"

> 1 John 4:17 (Amp.) ".... because as He is, so are we in this world."

Religion's gospel does NOT want us to be walking around acting like Jesus. Religion brings death, not life. So, religion's gospel needed to have just enough truth in it to sound authentic but just enough lies to keep us bound and powerless.

Lastly, there are no verses supporting the idea that Heaven starts when we die. Instead, this is what the Bible says eternal life is...

> John 17:3 (BSB) "Now this is eternal life, that they may know You, the only TRUE God, and Jesus Christ, whom You have sent."

Eternal life starts the moment we believe in Jesus. We become ONE with Jesus, seated in heavenly places, and co-heirs with Christ. This happens while we are here on earth... and eternal life happens even if we don't believe it happened yet! How short-changed would Jesus' death be if we couldn't be saved from sin here. What about the ABUNDANT life that the gospel talks about? Where is that in this "gospel"?

Myth 4:

In religion's gospel, there is always an undertone, an unspoken sense of Jesus and God having a good cop/bad cop relationship towards us. Jesus was the good cop trying to save us from eternal damnation, and God was the bad cop, full of wrath and punishment. In a twisted way, God the Father punished and poured His wrath out on His only son, that He loved. God is often described as the stoic, just, and holy judge, while Jesus is the personable, loving, sacrificial lamb.

WRONG! Jesus is the EXACT representation of the Father, as I noted in Myth 2. There is no good cop/bad cop complex in their relationship. In addition, God did not pour his wrath out on Jesus. Instead, Isaiah 53 states the opposite!

> Isaiah 53:3-6 (BSB) "He was despised and rejected by men, a man of sorrows, acquainted with grief. Like one from whom men hide their faces, He was despised, and we esteemed Him not. Surely, He took on our infirmities and carried our sorrows; yet _we considered Him stricken by God, struck down and afflicted._ But He was pierced for our transgressions, He was crushed for our iniquities; the punishment that brought us peace was upon Him, and by His stripes, we are healed. We all like sheep have gone astray, each one has turned to his own way, and the LORD has laid upon Him the iniquity of us all." [emphasis mine]

This is such an incredible passage. "...we considered Him stricken by God, struck down and afflicted...". There is no mention of God's wrath being poured out on Jesus in this passage or anywhere else that I can find. The only wrath we can extract from this passage is the wrath in OUR hearts that were blinded in sin. WE despised and rejected Jesus. We beat and tormented Him and then claimed that GOD was the one doing it to Jesus. What God was actually doing was laying every consequence of sin on Jesus. "...the Lord has laid upon Him the iniquity of us all." God did not pour His wrath out on Jesus who was coming to save the creation (that they both deeply loved)! At Jesus' choice and submission, Yahweh did give Jesus the full weight of sin SO THAT Jesus could break its power over us. It wouldn't have been right for Jesus to choose to sin because He would have been subject to it. Instead, Jesus stayed yielded to the Father in every moment. This is why the Father had to be the one to lay the consequence of sin on Him.

"...He was pierced for our transgressions; He was crushed for our iniquities; the punishment that brought us peace was upon Him..." The word "for" in this passage is a poor translation. When studying Hebrew in context, it would be more accurately translated as "because of". "He was pierced BECAUSE OF our transgressions...BECAUSE OF our iniquities..." WE were the ones crushing and beating Jesus. It WAS a punishment, but it wasn't a punishment from God to Jesus. It was "because of" our hearts being blinded by sin that WE punished Jesus to appease our own wrathful hearts. WE hated Truth. WE despised Him. WE rejected Him...all because of the death and the blindness we were wrapped in. Yahweh does not desire punishment. He is not a God who wants us to suffer because we broke the rules. Does He discipline? Yes, of course He does. Discipline is what every good parent does to EMPOWER their child to make better choices. Without discipline, there can be no maturity. So, it is the kindness of a parent to discipline their child to help them grow so they can be powerful adults. Discipline is very different than punishment and suffering. Suffering comes from Satan. Satan causes us to suffer in sin, and then he tricks us into believing that God did it! Satan scapegoats God and tries to convince us that the Father is the kind of God who is full of wrath and makes sinners suffer.

It's vitally important to see that sin punishes us, not God. Sin causes separation, not God. WE turned our face, not God. Blinded by sin, WE poured our wrath out on Jesus, not God. And then we blamed God for what we did to Jesus on the cross. And as we poured our brokenness and death out on Jesus, He took every bit of it and said, "I am going to use this for your healing and restoration. I will take all this on and trade my life with yours so you can be free." It's the most beautiful and powerful thing in all of the universe. And sin and death couldn't stop it.

Myth 5:

This life is about biding our time on earth until we can escape through death or until Jesus comes back and saves us from the horribleness.

Escapism is the undertone in religion's gospel that encourages you to just bide your time till you can escape this terrible world and go to Heaven. Your eyes are longingly looking to Heaven, waiting for the day "you'll finally be out of pain". This concept is totally backwards! Adam and Eve weren't told to just bide their time in the garden. They were called to transform the whole earth to look like the garden. Their job was to bring Heaven to earth and reign like Jesus over the earth. Dying was never a part of the picture and neither was escaping to Heaven! And the message didn't change when Jesus came. Jesus NEVER mentioned dying and going to Heaven. We are ALREADY seated in Heaven when we choose Jesus (more on that later.) And we are called to bring Heaven to Earth as salt and light! Escaping from earth was never the plan and yet somehow escapism has been twisted into religion's gospel.

Myth 6:

If you try hard enough, you will arrive at some spiritual level and maybe gain God's approval for a moment. There are spiritual goals for us to strive towards, and maybe with lots of work, we will finally "arrive".

Arrivism is the undertone in religion's gospel that promises "one day you'll get there". Arrivism has goals and false finish lines. For example, "I'll be a mature Christian when I raise someone from the dead". This was literally what I thought, that I would have succeeded at some level of spirituality when I raised someone from the dead. If you think that at some point you will "arrive" in your walk with the Lord, then you have been misled. The point of the journey is the journey. It's not about arriving to Heaven one day—you're already there. It's not about arriving at some spiritual level—there is ALWAYS more to learn and grow in. Yahweh is infinite. We can never and will never "arrive". The whole point of the gospel, which we are just about to dive into, is relational. In a relationship, it's not about "arriving". It's our living each moment together through the seasons and ages. The only thing you can "arrive" at, happened the moment you chose Jesus. You've already arrived because you have joined the love dance with Jesus for all eternity.

There is much more evidence of the twistedness of religion's gospel. I hope you begin to question what you were taught and seek out what the Bible actually says. Religion brings death, and it has infiltrated the church. It's time to set the record straight and set a good foundation.

This is how I would _roughly_ summarize the good news according to the Bible:

Father, Son, and Holy Spirit were in a blissful, abundant, and perfect union before time and space. The Greeks called it— perichoresis. Perichoresis is a dance of perfect union and timing where the dancers seem to be one. THAT is how the Greeks were able to explain the Godhead—three in one in perfect harmony. And it was in that harmony that Father, Jesus, and Holy Spirit decided they wanted to expand the family. So they created everything from that desire.

> *Ephesians 1:4-5 (NLT) "Even before he made the world, God loved us and chose us in Christ to be holy and without fault in his eyes. God decided in advance to adopt us into his own family by bringing us to himself through Jesus Christ. This is what he wanted to do, and it gave him great pleasure."*

> *John 1:1-4 (NLT) "In the beginning the Word already existed. The Word was with God, and the Word was God. He existed in the beginning with God. God created everything through him, and nothing was created except through him. The Word gave life to everything that was created, and his life brought light to everyone."*

They created mankind in their very own image. Man was given the earth to rule and reign over so he could transform the whole earth to look like heaven (the Eden model).

> *Genesis 1:26-28 (BSB) "Then God said, "Let Us make man in Our image, after Our likeness, to rule over the fish of the sea and the birds of the air, over the livestock, and over all the earth itself and every creature that crawls upon it." So God created man in His own image; in the image of God He created him; male and female He created them. God blessed them and said to them, "Be fruitful and multiply, and fill the earth and subdue it; rule over the fish of the sea and the birds of the air and every creature that crawls upon the earth."*

Man was also given free will because free will is the only way to have true love. If man were a robot, none of man's choices would be genuine. God wanted free kids to be able to choose what they wanted. And with that freedom, Adam and Eve chose to not follow God's ways. They ate from the tree of knowledge of good and evil. Their eyes were opened to good and evil, judgment, and sin. They judged themselves and hid because they felt unworthy. Sin DOES bring death and separation, BUT it is because we separate ourselves from God. And any separation from God equals death. The whole concept of sin is presented differently in the Bible than in how I was taught:

> 2 Corinthians 5:19 (BSB) "that God was reconciling the world to Himself in Christ, not counting men's trespasses against them. And He has committed to us the message of reconciliation."

> John 3:17 (BSB) "For God did not send his Son to condemn the world, but to save the world through Him."

After they sinned, YAHWEH STILL CAME TO THE GARDEN. And Yahweh did not come with wrath and lightning bolts. God came to walk with Adam, and ADAM hid from God. God doesn't NEED blood to be appeased. It's never been about sacrifices or blood to try and please God and subdue His wrath. Even King David understood that in the Old Testament BEFORE Jesus came! It's never been about burnt sacrifice; it's always been about our hearts.

> Psalm 51:16 (NLT) "You do not desire a sacrifice, or I would offer one. You do not want a burnt offering."

Sin is a big deal, but it's a big deal because of what it does to us—not because it's a judgment issue. Sin is a big deal because we pull away from Yahweh, not the other way around. Jesus came for the lost, the blind, and the sick. He came to save us from our sins and death so that we could be made new creations and be called sons of God. Yahweh laid the sins of the world on Jesus, but that is a very different thing than God pouring His wrath on Jesus. The Bible says WE were the ones who tried to kill him, not God's wrath. Sin blinds and binds us in a sticky trap. Because of sin-filled hearts, we hated Jesus when He was on the earth. That hatred grew into a murderous heart that tried to kill Jesus. Then to top things off, we blamed Yahweh for what WE did to Jesus! Even crazier, Isaiah said all this would happen BEFORE Jesus came!

> *Isaiah 53:3-6 (BSB) "He was despised and rejected by men, a man of sorrows, acquainted with grief. Like one from whom men hide their faces, He was despised, and we esteemed Him not. Surely, He took on our infirmities and carried our sorrows; yet we considered Him stricken by God, struck down and afflicted. But He was pierced for our transgressions, He was crushed for our iniquities; the punishment that brought us peace was upon Him, and by His stripes, we are healed. We all like sheep have gone astray, each one has turned to his own way, and the LORD has laid upon Him the iniquity of us all."*

> *2 Corinthians 5:21 (BSB) "God made Him who knew no sin to be sin on our behalf, so that in Him we might become the righteousness of God."*

Jesus couldn't just take away our sin. We would just sin again in our brokenness. We needed a total transformation, not just a wiping of the slate. When we believe in Jesus, we become a new creation- from human to a son of God. We changed species forever; there's no way to go back. From that point on, we are no longer human and are an alien to this world. No longer slaves, but saints. Literally ONE with God Himself. We are co-crucified and co-risen with Jesus. And we MIGHT sin, but if we do, it is not our identity anymore. A king might act like a pauper, but acting like a pauper can't change the king's identity. Our identity is forever and fully changed because of Christ. Period. There is nothing we can do to add to that or undo what Jesus has done. We are just like Jesus in our ability and in how the Father sees and loves us.

> *2 Corinthians 5:16-18 (BSB) "So from now on we regard no one according to the flesh. Although we once regarded Christ in this way, we do so no longer. Therefore if anyone is in Christ, he is a new creation. The old has passed away. Behold, the new has come! All this is from God, who reconciled us to Himself through Christ and gave us the ministry of reconciliation."*

> *1 Corinthians 6:17 (ESV) "But he who is joined to the Lord becomes one spirit with him."*

> *Ezekiel 36:26 (BSB) "I will give you a new heart and put a new spirit within you; I will remove your heart of stone and give you a heart of flesh."*

> *1 John 4:17 (ESV) "...as he is, so we are in this world." (Note: This verse is written after Jesus' ascension—so it is referring to how He is NOW)*

> *Ephesians 2:6 (NLT) "For he raised us from the dead along with Christ and seated us with him in the heavenly realms because we are united with Christ Jesus."*

So now, having this new identity IN Christ, one with Him, what's the endgame? What's the point? If we aren't waiting to die until we can go to Heaven to sit in the clouds with Jesus, what is this all about? God doesn't need our money. He doesn't need slave labor. He also doesn't need our worship. God doesn't NEED anything actually.

He wanted a family, and it gave Him great pleasure to make a family. And being a part of God's family is the BEST thing ever. The joy, the peace, the life, the rest, the adventure, the FUN... it's all so incredible! The good news of the gospel is GOOD. We are invited to join in the eternal love dance with Yahweh Himself. The commandments in the Bible describe who we already are. ALL of the mandates in the Bible are "get to's," not "have to's". They are COmmands intended to be done together with Jesus. When we become ONE with Jesus, we become the embodiment of Love himself. We ARE love. The law was fulfilled in Jesus, and now there is NO condemnation.

> Romans 8:1-4 (TPT) "So now the case is closed. There remains no accusing voice of condemnation against those who are joined in life-union with Jesus, the Anointed One. For the "law" of the Spirit of life flowing through the anointing of Jesus has liberated us from the "law" of sin and death. For God achieved what the law was unable to accomplish, because the law was limited by the weakness of human nature. Yet God sent us his Son in human form to identify with human weakness. Clothed with humanity, God's Son gave his body to be the sin-offering so that God could once and for all condemn the guilt and power of sin. So now every righteous requirement of the law can be fulfilled through the Anointed One living his life in us. And we are free to live, not according to our flesh, but by the dynamic power of the Holy Spirit!"

> 1 Corinthians 10:23 (AMP) "All things are lawful [that is, morally legitimate, permissible], but not all things are beneficial or advantageous. All things are lawful, but not all things are constructive [to character] and edifying [to spiritual life]."

We have the best deal and opportunity in all of the universe. We are one spirit with Him in perfect union and bliss! We bring Heaven and the ministry of reconciliation everywhere we go. Creation is waiting eagerly for us to free them from the curse of sin. Everything we do can flow from friendship and rest in oneness with Jesus. We aren't waiting to die so we can escape to Heaven. Eternal life started the moment we chose Jesus. We are in eternity NOW, and God has commissioned us as ambassadors to transform the whole earth to look like our home—Heaven! There is an alternative to the pain, sickness, and death. That IS good news!

Chapter Two:

OUR NEW IDENTITY

So, who are we then if we aren't what religion told us? Do you realize that Jesus never called us "Christians"? Our identity went from being a human to a "Son of God." As humans, we had a heart of stone, were lost, blind, and rebellious against the things of God. That old man is gone now, never to come back again. We are NEW creations, a new class of being (son of God) that is ONE with Jesus Himself. The term "Christian" is a label that was given to us by <u>unbelievers</u> in Antioch (Acts 11:26). The world's institution didn't have a grid for the new class of being that we were, so it called us "Christians". What was once about relationship (being a son of God) slowly became focused on do- ing the actions and duties of a "Christian." Religion's institution crept in and made *doing* things more important than growing the RELATIONSHIP we were created for.

That is why being a "Christian" can be such a trap. Yes, a trap. What a "Christian" is and *should* look like changes <u>drastically</u> from church to church (and culture to culture). For example, some churches say that to be a "good Christian," we *should* sing and dance in worship. But then the church across the street says that "good Christians" *should* sit and be reverent in worship. So, which is correct? <u>Neither of them</u>. Jesus is the same yesterday, today, and forever. His intention has always been to be RELA- TIONAL with us, not engaging with us for what we can do or give Him. In the garden, He was relational. In the flesh, He was relational, and still to this day, Jesus wants RELATIONSHIP! The disciples themselves wanted to know how to DO the things of God. They were used to religious institutions that demand ser- vice and actions, so they asked Jesus how they could adhere to the demands they thought existed. And this was His reply...

John 6:28-29 (NLT) "They replied, 'We want to perform God's works, too. What should we do?' Jesus told them, 'This is the only work God wants from you: Believe in the one he has sent.'"

"Believe in the one he has sent." The disciples asked for religious demands. Instead, Jesus told them to engage their hearts. Our new identity does not revolve around actions and doing. We are SONS of the Most High, first and foremost. (Then after we develop who we are, we naturally will act in our true nature and bring Heaven to Earth in all we do!) An easy way to tell the difference between religion and relationship is this: religion cares about the outward appearance, but relationship with God looks at the heart. Now, let's explore some verses that dismantle what religion has said and see what the Bible actually says about us! Read them slowly and take them in...

God made and calls us GOOD, not a wretch:

Genesis 1:31 (BSB) "And God looked upon all that He had made, and indeed, it was very good." [Emphasis mine]

Ephesians 1:4-5 (NLT) "Even before he made the world, God loved us and chose us in Christ to be holy and without fault in his eyes. God decided in advance to adopt us into his own family by bringing us to himself through Jesus Christ. This is what he wanted to do, and it gave him great pleasure." [Emphasis mine]

Genesis 1:27 (BSB) "So God created man in his own image, in the image of God he created him; male and female he created them."

Psalm 139:14 (ESV) "I praise you, for I am fearfully and wonderfully made. Wonderful are your works; my soul knows it very well."

Ephesians 2:10 (ESV) "For we are his workmanship, created in Christ Jesus for good works, which God prepared beforehand, that we should walk in them."

Note: Yahweh does not create wretches or broken things. Everything He creates is GOOD, PLEASING, BEAUTIFUL, and INTENTIONAL.

We were lost and blind:

Ephesians 2:13 (BSB) "But now in Christ Jesus you who once were far off have been brought near by the blood of Christ." [Emphasis mine]

Ephesians 5:8 (ESV) "For at one time you were darkness, but now you are light in the Lord. Walk as children of light." [Emphasis mine]

Ephesians 4:22-24 (ESV) "to put off your old self, which belongs to your former manner of life and is corrupt through deceitful desires, and to be renewed in the spirit of your minds, and to put on the new self, created after the likeness of God in true righteousness and holiness."

Ezekiel 36:26 (BSB) "I will give you a new heart and put a new spirit within you; I will remove your heart of stone and give you a heart of flesh." [Emphasis mine. Also, note this verse says "will give" because it was a promise from the Old Testament of what Jesus was going to do and is now what we walk in!]

Romans 5:8 (ESV) "But God demonstrates his own love for us in this: While we were still sinners, Christ died for us." [Emphasis mine]

Note: We were lost and blind and sick. But that's not who God created us to be and not who we are once we choose Jesus.

We are now:

Galatians 3:26 (ESV) "For in Christ Jesus you are all sons of God, through faith." [Emphasis mine]

Galatians 3:28 (ESV) "There is neither Jew nor Greek, there is neither slave nor free, there is no male and female, for you are all one in Christ Jesus." [Emphasis mine]

John 15:15 (ESV) "No longer do I call you servants, for the servant does not know what his master is doing; but I have called you friends, for all that I have heard from my Father I have made known to you." [Emphasis mine]

1 Peter 2:9 (ESV) "But you are a chosen race, a royal priesthood, a holy nation, a people for his own possession, that you may proclaim the excellencies of him who called you out of darkness into his marvelous light." [Emphasis mine]

1 Corinthians 12:27 (ESV) "Now you are the body of Christ and individually members of it." [Emphasis mine]

1 Corinthians 6:17 (ESV) "But he who is joined to the Lord becomes one spirit with him."

1 John 3:1 (ESV) "See what kind of love the Father has given to us, that we should be called children of God; and so we are." [Emphasis mine]

Ephesians 2:19 (ESV) "So then you are no longer strangers and aliens, but you are fellow citizens with the saints and members of the household of God." [Emphasis mine]

1 John 4:17 (ESV) "...as he is, so we are in this world." [Emphasis mine]

We have:

> *1 Corinthians 2:16 (NLT) "'For, Who can know the LORD's thoughts? Who knows enough to teach him?' But we understand these things, for we have the mind of Christ." [Emphasis mine]*

> *1 Peter 2:24 (NLT) "He personally carried our sins in his body on the cross so that we can be dead to sin and live for what is right. By his wounds, you are healed." [Emphasis mine]*

> *Ephesians 2:6 (NLT) "For he raised us from the dead along with Christ and seated us with him in the heavenly realms..." [Emphasis mine]*

> *Ephesians 1:3 (ESV) "Blessed be the God and Father of our Lord Jesus Christ, who has blessed us in Christ with every spiritual blessing in the heavenly places." [Emphasis mine]*

> *Note: Notice the past tense in these verses. It's done. Not by your power or good works, but freely and fully given to you!*

These verses are talking about us! They describe and explain who we ARE! Our true identity as a son of God was decided and paid for at the foundations of the earth. It does not change even in the midst of poor choices and actions. A son is a son regardless of how he acts. If a child acts like a cat, does that change the identity of the child into a cat? Obviously not. Our actions cannot change who we are! Jesus' plan of redemption is bigger than any action or mistake we could make.

I hope that you really take the time to absorb the verses in this chapter. Read them over and over until your heart believes them. I suggest you ask Jesus about each one individually. Ask Him to tell you what they mean and how they apply to your life. The Word is filled with verses that clearly lay out the gospel and who we are. I pray that you question what religion has taught you. Religion is the enemy, a liar, and a thief. There is so much more for us than what we are walking in. The gospel is not dull, and we definitely do not need to wait to die before we experience ABUNDANT LIFE! When we become hungry for the abundant life that we already have, that is the beginning of our journey of transformation.

Chapter Three:

THE PROCESS OF TRANSFORMATION

So, we get saved. We chose Jesus, and now we are one with Him. SO much has changed...but not everything has changed. We still feel offended, depressed, or afraid, but how? If Jesus isn't afraid or offended, and we are one with Him, then what's going on? Half of the New Testament says things like "it is finished"; "we are new creations", or "we are seated in Heavenly places". Then the other half makes it seem like it's not done in verses like "take your thoughts captive"; "strive to enter into His rest", or "renew your mind so you will transform your life". So, is it done, or is it not done? Is it finished or do we have to do something? THAT is the question we will answer in this chapter.

Physical   **Spiritual**
Body   **Soul**   **Spirit**

We are three-part, multi-dimensional beings. One part is visible (our body), one part is *partly* visible (our soul), and one part is invisible (our spirit). Souls are measurable in the form of electricity, so that is why I credit them as *partly* visible. These three parts make up our being, regardless of our understanding of their reality, role, and process.

Our body is the easiest part to describe. It is the part of us that we are most familiar with and is the part that we are regularly conscious of. Our body enables us to be the hands and voice of Heaven or Hell on this earth. Most of our cognitive life is spent over-focusing on our body that exists in the third dimension. Though our spirit and soul are just as much a part of us, most people are unaware of them. This is why we are so agreeable to the enemy and his schemes because his tactics target our souls.

Our spirit is our living body in the spirit world. It cannot be disabled or damaged, and as a believer, it is the part of us that is ONE spirit with Jesus. The moment we chose Jesus, our spirit changed forever by joining with God Himself in the eternal love dance! All of the verses mentioned in the last chapter explain the reality already in our spirit. It IS finished. We ARE a new creation and seated in Heavenly places. The "We Have" and "We Are" sections in chapter 2 are the current reality our spirit lives in now with Jesus.

Now for the SOUL. The soul is the connection between our body and our spirit—it is the bridge between two dimensions! The soul is also the part of us that is our free will, thoughts, and emotions. When we are born, our soul is the one in charge. Our destiny, and the reality we walk in, is decided by our soul's beliefs. The soul is the part that WE are responsible for in the process of transformation because it is where our free will is. I'll explain. The moment we were saved, our spirit became ONE spirit with Christ. We changed identities permanently. We were powerless to save ourselves. We needed a savior and a total transformation. And Jesus delivered! We got the best deal in all the universe: To be ONE spirit with God himself and join in the eternal love dance! But God still didn't want robots. Somehow Jesus had to preserve our free will. So, Jesus offers to become one with us and give us His own Spirit, and that empowers us with everything we need. Our oneness with Christ is our abundance, our wholeness, our victory, our strength, and our anchor. So, Jesus SAVED us and empowers us in our spirit while at the same time Jesus preserved our free choice in our souls. So now, we are empowered by JESUS in our spirits to do all things, BUT it is our choice to choose in every moment in every area in our souls. It is truly brilliant how Jesus saved us while also preserving our free will.

So, the verses mentioned in the last chapter are 100% true! While at the SAME time, these verses are 100% relevant as well!

- *"...we take every thought captive to make it obedient to Christ..."* 2 Corinthians 10:5 (BSB)

- *"...Be transformed by the renewing of your mind..."* Romans 12:2 (NKJV)

- Or *"...make every effort to enter into that rest..."* Hebrews 4:11 (BSB)

There is never conflict in the scriptures, we just need a revelation into what God is saying! He is that big and that good to be able to totally save and empower us while at the same time preserve our free will! When we renew our minds, that's when the power of being one with Jesus in our spirit flows out of our soul and body. Renewing our mind is when we change the way we think and view life—from a human perspective to a son of God perspective.

There is already power in our spirit. The key is our soul. Our soul decides if it is going to agree with the power and reality in our spirit or if it will agree with pain and the message from human thinking. The more your soul agrees with what is done in our spirit, the more our soul and body will be transformed by the life that is already there. Trauma, pain, and believing lies affect our soul like bacteria infects a wound. Unhealed pain will always begin to infect our soul and then impact our physical body. Dr. Caroline Leaf has been able to scientifically prove that our physical brain syncs with our soul 6x a minute! This syncing up aligns our physical body with whatever the soul believes, thinks, and feels. The brain releases either healing or destroying chemicals into our bodies based on our soul's health.

Think of the soul as having real estate. When your soul is badly wounded, brokenness and pain take up part of the real estate in your soul. This means that pain has the voting power in how we perceive and respond to life around us. If the majority of the real estate of our heart believes lies and is in pain, then pain and brokenness will ooze out. But if the majority of our heart is healed and believing truth, then we will act like the life-giving spirit that we already are. We won't be reacting to the world around us but will be powerfully affecting and shifting things in the world to look like Heaven.

Simply, it comes down to this: God is constantly saying one thing while Satan is saying the opposite. And, we are in the middle, deciding who we are going to believe. Unconsciously, we are deciding who we will believe moment by moment. I am challenging you to pay attention to your thoughts and be intentional with who you are agreeing with. If Satan can get us to agree with his lies, he can influence our thoughts, will, emotions, and actions even after we are saved. The more we believe what God says, the more our life is transformed by the abundant life that ALREADY exists in our spirit that is one with Jesus. We have everything that Jesus has: perfect peace, a solution for everything, wholeness (the step beyond healing), wisdom beyond the ages, unlimited provision, and so much more! It's already done in our spirit; our soul is the one we have to convince. And that convincing starts as blind FAITH.

Choosing to have faith is harder than it sounds though. To a broken and hurting soul, Truth sounds foreign and even offensive. It requires faith to choose to believe something that we don't even have a grid for. Our soul remembers the past and the pain of this broken world. Our soul FEELS like the lies of shame or rejection are justified. Our soul FEELS like the lies of a poverty mindset are true. Our soul FEELS like control and walls are helpful and good at protecting us from more pain. But our soul is wrong. Dead wrong. Our soul is trying to make sense of a broken world and the lies from the enemy make "sense" when we are in pain and blind.

Renewing the mind is simple to explain yet difficult to walk out. If getting free from our pain and bondages were easy, then everyone would be doing it. Nobody WANTS to live in pain, yet most are too comfortable, or afraid, to face their pain. THAT is the difficult part. To be free and healed, we must face our greatest torments on blind faith that Jesus is big enough to handle each and every one. It is incredibly hard and even terrifying to face our pain and demons. I know because I have been there many times in many different ways. BUT I can tell you, allowing Jesus to heal our deepest wounds is always worth the cost and fear of facing them! Jesus IS big enough and He is who He says He is. Being on the other side of the pain and seeing the freedom and life that is available to me was absolutely worth the cost of facing my pain and fear.

I have endured sexual abuse. I have experienced a miscarriage and other great loss. I spent years dealing with night terrors, rejection, betrayal, and great heartache of many kinds. I had a total psychiatric breakdown and had triggers both physically and emotionally. I felt like I had been to hell and back multiple times, but you know what? I experienced those things, but I do not carry them or their scars. I am NOT a victim and the pain I once had is NOT my identity. I share these things to give weight to what I am writing about. You can be whole. NOTHING that we face is greater than Jesus' ability to heal us and make us whole. And to be fully clear, part of you is ALREADY whole… your soul just doesn't believe it yet.

Jesus is whole, and you are one with Him. Jesus isn't sick, so you have been healed. He isn't lacking anything, so you are in abundance at this moment. There is no darkness in Him, so you too are filled with light and wholeness. To a soul in pain, these statements are offensive and painful to read. But if you choose to push through those feelings of offense and pain, then you can start your healing journey OUT of the dark and pain you feel.

Most people stop when they feel the offense and pain. They check out and want to put the pain back in the box that they had it in before they were triggered. But here's the thing, that pain was already there to that magnitude and it will continue to be there until you address it.

Triggers reveal inward realities that were once contained; it was always there or we wouldn't have been triggered! So, as challenging as it is, every trigger is actually a precious invitation into freedom! Things that were buried deep, some of which we may not have even known were hiding in the basement of our soul, come to light when we are triggered. Each time this happens, if we bring the trigger to Jesus, then it's a beautiful opportunity to be freed of pain that was once hidden! Where the enemy meant to trigger and crush us, Jesus uses it for our breakthrough and healing!

This journey is not easy, but it is possible because of Jesus. It is incredibly hard to face our pain and choose to believe something that is opposite to our experience. It FEELS like the enemy is telling the truth. When we start this journey, what Jesus says to us doesn't make sense because our souls are blinded and deafened when in pain. How can there be enough when we have seen so much lack? How am I healed when I still feel pain? How can there be joy for mourning? How is fear lying? Satan has spent our whole lives trying to convince us that his lies are fact. Not only that, but we are often so deceived in our pain that it becomes our friend or comfort. Depression feels like the dark friend that's always there. Control or anger are "helpers" in navigating a big, scary world. Poverty "helps" us be "wise" with money. The list goes on and on.

Before Jesus, all we have experienced is brokenness and pain in this world. From our conception, we have known lack, pain, and sickness. We eat, sleep, and breathe it in all around us. Broken people twisted the gospel to make sense of the pain and brokenness of the world. To believe what Jesus says challenges everything we have ever known. It was easier to twist the gospel than be challenged out of our pain. Jesus says there is always enough. Jesus says we are healed. He says we are already blessed with every spiritual blessing, but we haven't experienced any of that yet. Every truth and concept of the Kingdom is beyond this natural world. What Jesus says is opposite to "natural" laws because He teaches and lives from a HIGHER reality...and He is inviting us to live in that higher reality with Him. Many people stay stuck in their souls after they get saved because they aren't willing or don't know how to fully entrust everything to Jesus. The more we choose to believe what Jesus says over the lies of the enemy, the more healing and supernatural things we will see.

In my life, I have faced great pain. Some pain I faced without trusting Jesus, and some pain I faced believing what He says. And the difference was staggering. I had my share of trauma and carried it with me everywhere I went. Its festering pain affected every area of my life until I encountered Jesus for the first time. When I started a personal relationship with Jesus, He retroactively healed the pain in my past and all its negative effects! His healing was so powerful that He even healed the memories of trauma. Now when I look back at those memories, all I see is Jesus smiling back at me. To make things even more incredible, Jesus taught me how to walk through pain WITH Him. Jesus is big enough to heal moment by moment in painful times! Instead of being broken by the world, I was in the valley of darkness with Light and Healing Himself. Jesus doesn't promise an easy or pain-free life. He actually guarantees there will be hard times, especially for believers. But in everything we face, He spins it on its head and makes all things work out for good. He has a solution and is big enough for every single thing we experience. So we can walk through the valley of darkness and not fear, because He is always there, one with us, fighting for us and bringing Light into the darkest places.

> John 16:33 (BSB) "I have told you these things
> so that in Me you may have peace. In the world
> you will have tribulation. But take courage; I have
> overcome the world!"

Jesus and Satan both know what happened at the resurrection. It's clearly understood in the spiritual realm who we are and what we already carry because of Jesus. The only ones figuring it out… are us. And THAT is the journey of transformation. The journey is beginning to choose to agree with what Jesus says and what He has already done. The journey is us finally deciding that Satan is a liar and everything he does and says is to destroy us, and then to decide that Jesus is speaking Truth. Moment by moment our soul has the free choice to agree with Satan's lies or Jesus' truth. And what we choose to believe each moment decides the reality our soul lives in and what happens in the world around us. It's a powerful thing. In fact, Jesus recently told me that there is nothing more powerful in all the universe than a "yes" for Jesus. Equally so, there is nothing more destructive than a "no" against Him. Each and every moment, we decide WHO we will believe and then we affect the world around us based on who we are believing.

So HOW can we know what our soul believes? Where do we start in this journey of renewing our mind? There are languages by which our soul communicates that reveal what our soul believes. However, most of us don't recognize or understand our soul's communication. Our physical body, our soul, and our spirit all are communicating in great detail. Below is a list of ways the soul communicates. As we learn to understand our soul's communication, we will be able to bring things to Jesus for Him to heal and speak Truth into.

The language of THOUGHT

Our thoughts are the first to reveal what we truly believe in our hearts. Our thoughts are powerful and critical in affecting our lives for good or evil. There's a pattern:

Our thoughts → become action.

Our actions → become a habit.

Our habits → become our destiny.

Our thoughts affect every area of our lives AND the world around us. Our thoughts reveal our soul's core beliefs and that is why we are told to take EVERY thought captive and make them obey Christ. It is vitally important to pay attention to what we think!

The language of FEELINGS

Our feelings and emotions are not bad! They are God-given indicators of what's going on in our souls. Our feelings and emotions are the thermometers that tell us the health of our souls. The feeling is not the bad guy. Feelings just expose how our heart is doing and who it is agreeing with. If we are feeling alone for example, it shows that we are believing the lie that we are alone. It also means that we don't believe we are one with Jesus and Yahweh in a Holy Spirit eternal dance.

The language of ACTION

Our actions reveal what we believe as well. Any time we don't act like Jesus, it reveals a part of our soul not walking in the health and fullness that God has for us. Whether it's using a substance to numb pain, lashing out verbally, or just being afraid to speak in front of people. Good or bad—every action reveals what our heart believes about itself, God, and the world around it.

To be transformed, we must pay attention to our soul's language and change our negative beliefs. The first step is to pay attention to what our soul is saying! The more we agree with what Jesus says, the more we are transformed. Once we decide that we are ready to face our pain and choose to push through the confrontation of its lies, then we will find Jesus there—big enough for every challenge and struggle. HIS strength is what carries us through. HE carries the burden. We simply agree with Him and what He has already done as we are intentional to face our deepest fears and pains.

> Revelation 3:20 "I stand at the door and knock, anyone who hears my voice AND opens the door. I will come in and have deep and blissful intimacy

with him and He with me." (Translation by author—
explained in next paragraph)

Most translations use the word "dine" instead of "deep and blissful intimacy". But the Greek word they are translating doesn't mean carnally eating food! The Greek word "deipneo" implies a deep and blissful intimacy shared between the best of friends or lovers. AND this verse was written to an established CHURCH. This verse and invitation to have deep and blissful intimacy was for BELIEVERS! Even as a believer, many people keep Jesus outside the walls of their hearts. Jesus is knocking on the door of our soul, waiting for us to not just hear His voice but to OPEN the door and let Him in. If we choose to, it will be the best and most blissful time ever, but the choice is up to us. So, what are you going to do? Will you let Jesus in and choose Him over the lies and pain?

Chapter Four:

ENGAGING WITH YAHWEH

Now for the HOW to renew our minds. The mind is an amazing tool that God carefully and skillfully crafted for us. It records everything that happens - both hurtful and joyful things. Amazingly, when we renew our minds and let Jesus heal us, even the hurtful things in our past can be redeemed and healed retroactively—physically and in our soul! There are multiple ways to go about renewing our minds and healing, but I will cover my favorite ways in this chapter.

There are two key factors in understanding renewing the mind.

1. First, renewing the mind is NOT something you can think yourself into. Head knowledge does not and cannot help our soul heal. Head "knowing" something without truly believing it just causes division and frustration to our soul. Religion gives us head knowledge without heart revelation and that is why we are left unchanged. I'll explain it this way, the brain makes decisions and functions based on what it sees in this third dimension. (Which by the way, you can only SEE about 1% of the light spectrum so there is a LOT you are not seeing.) Your soul is fourth-dimensional. So EVERYTHING your brain tries to convince your soul of will fall short. Head knowledge, brain "understanding", will never minister to or convince your soul of anything because it is operating

out of a lower dimension. Our soul needs a heart-to-heart encounter with Yahweh to be transformed and healed.

2. Second, to renew the mind, you MUST address (not deflect) wrong beliefs and thoughts. Let's say that this jar represents our mind and the balls represent our thoughts. When we have a thought, it's as if we focus on one of the balls in the jar. Now let's say that black balls are wrong thoughts. Most people try to change the way they think by choosing to not focus on a black ball and focus on a different one instead. They did change the focus of what they were thinking about BUT they did not <u>transform</u> the wrong thought. That black ball is still there, taking up residence in their mind. Deflection won't bring transformation. <u>The only way to RENEW our mind is to exchange that black ball for a new colored one from Jesus</u>.

Romans 12:2 (ESV) "Do not be conformed to this world, but be transformed by the renewal of your mind, that by testing you may discern what is the will of God, what is good and acceptable and perfect.

2 Corinthians 10:5 (ESV) "We destroy arguments and every lofty opinion raised against the knowledge of God, and take every thought captive to obey Christ"

EVERY thought needs to be challenged or tested against Truth. Many of our thoughts we know are "wrong" but there are many more thoughts that are equally wrong that we don't recognize. Many lies we are TOTALLY blind to until they are brought to the Light for testing. For example, religion has rebranded some fears by calling them "wisdom." Consequently, many of our thoughts that we would pass off as "wisdom" are actually fear—just rebranded. Lies rebranded as truth are possibly MORE damaging because we are oblivious to the destruction they cause. That is why we must take every thought to Jesus.

Bringing everything to Jesus is the key to renewing the mind. It's the first step. The strategy is that as we learn to bring everything to Jesus, we shift into ABIDING and love FROM that connection to Jesus. We have already joined the eternal love dance. But most of us live as orphans begging for scraps from religion's table. As we renew our minds, we will learn the truth about who we are and that will transfigure our life and the world around us. Now for my two favorite ways of renewing the mind...

Go on An Encounter

Encounter is the word I use to describe any conscious interaction we have with Jesus. I use the word "conscious" because we are constantly, unconsciously, interacting with God. In fact, we have spent our whole lives unconsciously interacting with God and the enemy—our souls just didn't realize it. Our spirit and God's spirit are ONE...so of course they will be constantly interacting! Our soul just hasn't learned to tune in to what's already happening in our spirit. Engaging with God, and consciously interacting with Him, trains our souls to tune into our inward reality. I call it an encounter but it could be referred to as prayer, engagement, etc., the name doesn't matter. Don't get caught up on semantics, the heart behind it is the same—we are choosing to consciously and intentionally connect with Jesus in a personal relationship. And having a close and personal relationship with Jesus is the single most important thing any believer can do.

It's a common lie for people to believe they can't hear or see God. How can that be if we are ONE with Him? Although we may not be able to see or hear Jesus with our physical bodies, our spirit is fully connected with Him. Our souls have spent most (or all) of our lives focusing on just one of the three dimensions we live in. We are all multi-dimensional beings with bodies in multiple dimensions at once. Our spirits are in the spirit world, now seated in Heavenly places (multiple) and our bodies are in the physical world.

> 2 Corinthians 4:18 (BSB) "So we fix our eyes not on what is seen, but on what is unseen. For what is seen is temporary, but what is unseen is eternal."
>
> 2 Corinthians 5:7 (BSB) "For we walk by faith, not by sight."
>
> Hebrews 11:1 (BSB) "Now faith is the assurance of what we hope for and the certainty of what we do not see."

The journey of transformation and even becoming a believer requires our soul to have FAITH in the spiritual world, its existence, and its greater reality. Encountering God shifts our soul's perspective and reality to be Heavenly minded and not earthly (carnally) minded. Our soul has shaped everything it believes around its experiences in the "taste, touch, see" world we live in. Our souls, blinded by pain and brokenness, decided how the world works and built beliefs around those ideas. We live within our soul's beliefs regardless if they are right or wrong.

That's why transforming the way we think is so vitally important. Our soul filters how we perceive the world around us based on the soul's belief system.

For example, if our soul believes that it can't hear or see God, then it acts a lot like this picture here. We <u>have</u> eyes and we <u>have</u> ears …We are just choosing to not listen or see, ONLY because we believe the <u>lie</u> that we can't hear or see Jesus. Our soul filters reality based on what it believes. If we believe we are rejected, we will live and experience rejection everywhere we go. On the flip side, if we believe we are loved, we will live and experience love everywhere we go—same reality, different beliefs. This is why our soul's beliefs are <u>vitally</u> important to correct and heal for our life to be transformed.

If we believe that we can't hear God, then we won't hear Him in most circumstances simply because <u>we</u> are blocking our hearing of Him (Just like the picture). That is our free choice though, not Jesus' desire. He is standing at the door knocking. Every lie our soul believes is a block that keeps us from living in Heaven's reality. As we choose to believe what Jesus says over the enemy's lies, what we see and experience <u>will</u> change because those blocks are getting removed. Every lie acts as a filter to our soul, much like what would happen if we wore a pair of sunglasses with purple lenses. EVERYTHING we saw around us would be purple. But is everything actually purple? No.

God is BIG enough to answer our biggest and scariest questions. He is WAITING to be invited into the darkest parts of our souls, so He can show us the truth and heal us! He wants us to be free from everything, from the smallest lie to the biggest and scariest things that haunt us. He's waiting, knocking on the door of our hearts, inviting us into a deep and blissful intimacy beyond our wildest dreams.

Usually, it is not audibly or physically that Jesus encounters us. Jesus is spirit and most of his interaction with us is in the invisible realm. Although He absolutely could reveal Himself in this world, there is a beauty and a preciousness in the faith we use to engage with Jesus in the spiritual realm. The spiritual realm is MORE real and even more tangible than this third-dimension world...we just haven't realized it yet. The more we live by the rules and reality of the spiritual realm, the more we will be able to break the rules and reality of this third dimension. Raising the dead, walking on water, and multiplying food is "impossible" in this world. In the spiritual realm though, it is elementary-level easy. [Hebrews 6:1-2] The spiritual realm supersedes this world in every way—its laws, realities, and its way of functioning. And the more we begin to live FROM that realm (that we already exist in), the more supernatural we will be in this world. All that to say, it is precious and GOOD for us to pursue engaging with Jesus in the spiritual realm instead of being offended that Jesus isn't audibly talking to us or physically showing up.

We can choose to trust Jesus even though we don't understand His methods. Jesus does things outside our minds intentionally. His ways won't make sense, especially when we first get to know Him because we are the least like Him at that point. The more we are on the journey of transformation though, the more whole we will become and His ways become less foreign...because they are becoming our ways as well! So, at first, it helps to choose to believe that Jesus knows best and does everything in our best interest, even if it offends us.

Additionally, I would encourage you to be patient and gracious with yourself. Learning to interact with an entirely new realm will take time and there will be a learning curve. It's an eternal love dance that we have joined and we won't "figure it all out" within the time frame we expect. Be patient with yourself; most of your life has been spent only being conscious and intentional with this world. In the same way we had to learn how to live in this world (talking, walking, adulting, etc.), there will be a process for us to learn as we live from the spiritual realm.

Meditation

I like to describe meditation as marinating. When we meditate, it is like we marinate in a certain concept or way of thinking. The longer we marinate in something, the more we take on the flavor of what we are meditating on. Meditation is effective and that's why it is mentioned again and again in the Bible.

> Psalms 119:15 (ESV) "I will meditate on your precepts and fix my eyes on your ways."
>
> Isaiah 26:3 (ESV) "You keep him in perfect peace whose mind is stayed on you, because he trusts in you."

Whether we realize it or not, we are already constantly meditating. The question is what are we meditating on? We can meditate on anything- good or bad. If we dwell on thoughts of lack, fear, or unforgiveness for example, then we are meditating on LIES from the enemy. Those lies will be the flavor we are marinating in and they will negatively affect our life. We can ruin a perfectly good steak if we marinate it in poison. Our soul decides what it is going to think about. When we choose to think about things of Heaven, it will flavor our thoughts, which will positively affect our life. The more we pay attention to our thoughts and become intentional with what we are meditating on, the quicker we will see change. Renewing our minds is not about stuffing and choosing to think about something else. It is marinating in the Word of God even in the face of opposing circumstances and accusations. By choosing to meditate on God's promises and truth, we are intentionally choosing to marinate in something good. That meditation in truth will begin to flavor our whole soul in healing and life and that will renew our mind!

Fathers and mothers of the faith were known for meditating day and night. Often their meditations were simple and short, but they allowed that simple and short phrase to consume and transform them. Even something short like "I am loved and I am the embodiment of Love" can radically transform our lives as we begin to assimilate that phrase as truth.

One of the easiest ways to be intentional with meditation is to listen to sermons or read a book on a specific subject. Find a speaker/author who you feel is in line with God's heart and listen to messages about the topic you are renewing your mind on. I have a list of speakers and messages in the Resources section in the back of the book. The sermons and books I shared are ones that I used personally to meditate on and renew my mind. While listening to a sermon or reading a book, I engaged with Yahweh to see how the things applied to my life. It was also helpful because Yahweh would sift out anything that wasn't for me. After listening to a sermon or reading a book, I would think about what was said and marinate in its teachings. For really good sermons, I would listen to them over and over again...and hear new things every time!

One difficult thing about meditation is simply REMEMBERING to do it! In the west, we are so busy so it can be helpful to set up reminders for yourself. A helpful key would be to consider HOW you learn best and pick reminders that best suit you. There are lots of ways to remind ourselves to be intentional about what we focus on. Here are some ideas that I found helpful:

- Set an alarm on your phone. When I really want to get something anchored in my heart, I will set an alarm to go off every hour (or half-hour) from 9 am-9 pm. Each time my alarm goes off, I intentionally focus my attention again on a specific verse or phrase. I do this until I see a shift in my thinking (or actions) that shows that I believe what I am meditating on. Is it extreme? Maybe. Does it work? Yes. If we focus our attention each hour on Truth, it absolutely will shift things. You don't have to do it every hour; it's just what I found to be helpful.

- Use physical reminders. Often, I change my phone background to be the phrase or truth I am meditating on. I also like to put sticky notes around the house and car. I have worn a rubber band around my hand or have drawn a phrase on my arm.

The ideas are limitless on how we can remind ourselves. Bottom line though, in my healing journey, I learned that it was important to meditate on truth and to continually engage with Jesus. These two things are what I have used in my personal journey of transformation and they are still what I use to this day. When I went on encounters, I was addressing wounds and lies in my soul. Then I would take the truth I learned and cling to it, meditate on it, until it became anchored in my soul. The habit of bringing things to Jesus became so normal that I began to do it continually. I now abide, live from, my oneness and connection with Yahweh instead of engaging Him only when I was hurting. Before you learn to abide though, it starts with becoming aware and intentional in your soul. Then you can grow your ability and focus to stay connected longer in your soul.

Chapter Five:

NUTS AND BOLTS OF ENGAGING WITH YAHWEH

This chapter is a list of tips and my best explanations of how to engage with the spiritual realm and encounter Yahweh. There is so much information on this topic—it's literally a whole new world. Imagine trying to break down this third dimension to someone in a two- dimension world. There's only so much you can explain. Eventually the person has to choose to engage with that realm to experience it for themselves. And that is my hope, that this book points you to Jesus and gives you the tools you need to engage with Jesus in a personal and real way. These next couple of chapters have a LOT of information packed into them. It took me over a decade to understand and navigate the tools in this book. So, I encourage you to take your time reading them, and go into it understanding that it will take time to process it all.

At first, choose a quiet place to practice engaging with Yahweh. Our brains are used to constant stimulation. Most people don't even go to the bathroom without their phones because their brains are trained (addicted actually) to the constant stimulation. It can be games, texts, or social media; it doesn't matter what we do on our phones. The point is that we have trained our brains to be constantly, and often mindlessly, doing something. So, I suggest choosing a place with little or no distractions to begin engaging or consciously focusing on God.

> Psalm 46:10 (BSB) "Be still and know that I am God..."
> Or the Passion Translation puts it this way: "Be silent
> and stop your striving and you will see that I am
> God..."

Being still, silent (in our thoughts too), and focusing our attention and intention on Jesus is the first place to start. Often it is difficult at first because our minds have not been trained to sit still. We are constantly scrolling or thinking. The good news is that the more we choose to be still and focus, the easier it will become.

Ask a question (or wait on Jesus) while intentionally focusing on Him. Remember, part of us is already one with Him, the difference is now we are being intentional to practice connecting with Him consciously. You continually direct your focus and thoughts on work, life, daydreams, fears, etc. Instead, you are choosing to direct your attention and focus on Jesus. As you choose to be still, you may only see black or a blank screen at first and that's ok. As you focus on Jesus, even without seeing Him, you can ask Him questions. Jesus may show you a picture or a whole scene (vision), much like the way we see dreams when we sleep or daydream. You may hear Jesus in your heart, similar to how you would have a conversation in your mind. This is the beginning practice of starting a personal relationship with Him in your soul. Some great questions you can ask are:

- What would you like to tell me today?

- What would you like to show me today?

- What would you like to heal in my heart today?

- What would you like to tell me about... (dream, event, person, etc.)?

It's also equally wonderful and powerful to just wait on Yahweh and sit quietly in His presence. Sometimes He speaks and sometimes there is healing and breakthrough that comes from being still in His presence.

LISTEN to what He says! So simple, yet SO hard to walk out. We have been trained in religion to do all the talking. Religion teaches us to "pray" without ever listening. And most of the time, it's not even praying. It's demanding or whining about our pain and discomfort. So instead, when choosing to go on an encounter—LISTEN to what He is saying. This is part of being STILL. Ask a question and LISTEN. Or just wait on Jesus without even asking something, just focus on Him.

How do I know I'm not making it up? This is all SO foreign to us at first. Your mind most likely will scream, "This is crazy! This isn't real! (Or my favorite) This sounds like a cult.". I have been there, and sometimes I still question the crazy part! Everything in the Kingdom is so different from the world around us—it IS crazy to this world and worldly thinking! BUT there is GOOD fruit here! Fruit that remains!

> 1 John 4:1 (BSB) "Beloved, do not believe every spirit, but test the spirits to see whether they are from God. For many false prophets have gone out into the world."

I was so incredibly broken in my soul. I believed so many lies and was so insecure. I was a mess even though I was deeply religious. Religion didn't get me out of my pain—I thought I had to suffer through this life until I died before I could have ETERNAL and ABUNDANT life. Everything changed when I started a personal relationship with Jesus at winter camp. Jesus became real, personal, and tangible to me. As I allowed Him to, Jesus healed my pain and corrected the lies that were holding me back. THAT is good fruit. What we are doing is backed by the Word. Even in the Old Testament, God wanted a personal relationship with us. And several people chose to engage with God and say "yes" to Him even if it was scary or challenged everything they knew. God walked with Adam. Abraham was friends with God. Moses went up the mountain to see God. The Israelites were invited to go too but they chose not to because they were afraid! King David was a man after God's heart. Enoch and Elijah believed in Truth to the point that they did not die—instead, they and their bodies were raptured! Many mighty men and women engaged with Yahweh, even before Jesus came. These fathers and mothers of the faith all had a personal relationship with God. Yahweh is not distant. He wants a close and personal relationship with each and every one of His kids.

To answer the original question "How do I know I'm not making this up?" ...most likely you won't know if you are making it up or not at first. It requires FAITH and faith is the confidence in what we hope for and assurance about what we do not see. Like I have said before, most people spend their lives conscious of only this world—often ignorant of the soul and usually ignorant of their spirit and the spiritual realm. To believe there is a whole other realm (and part of you that already exists in that realm) is BEYOND this world...literally by definition. It will most likely feel crazy and like you are making it up at first. So, in faith, you chose to believe Jesus and you choose to begin a personal relationship with Him. Over time, as your soul heals and experiences Yahweh, you will see a change for the good. Your thoughts, feelings, and emotions change as you agree more and more with Jesus and Truth. You'll have more peace, joy, courage, and health.

You will also begin to notice that things you see and hear in encounters are beyond you. You will hear smarter thoughts, deeper concepts, or see pictures of things you would have never imagined yourself. For example, a friend of mine was struggling to know if the encounter was real or not and Jesus told her a word that she didn't know the definition of. When we looked up the word, it was EXACTLY what she needed to hear, but neither of us knew the word! Jesus will surprise you and wants to connect with you in a personal way. I encourage you to NOT let the thought "I'm making this up" come between you and connecting with Jesus. Now that we confirmed that you probably will think you are making it up at first, I want to give you some tips on how to start...

While consciously engaging with God, remember:

1. **Ask questions in your encounter!** When talking with God, be child-like and ask "Why?" until you are satisfied. Play 20 questions with Jesus whenever He tells you or shows you something.

   > *Proverbs 25:2 (BSB) "It is the glory of God to conceal things, but the glory of kings to search them out"*

   By design, God doesn't make all things known when He shows us visions. That would remove the relationship side of the encounter! He wants us to dig and ask questions and connect with Him. And it's FUN that way! We get to learn more about Him when we ask "Why?". Scavenger hunts would be no fun if everything was in plain sight. God purposefully hides things for us to find in encounters.

2. **Talk with the whole Godhead.** In an encounter, your soul is consciously choosing to focus on Father, Jesus, or Holy Spirit and talk with Him. It's ideal to have a healthy relationship with ALL of the Godhead. So go on encounters with Father God, Holy Spirit, and Jesus. You can go with all three of them at once or go on different encounters with each one separately. If you have never met or had an encounter with one of the parts of the Godhead, ask the part of the Godhead you are familiar with to introduce you to the other members. I suggest when you meet a new part of the Godhead, ask them questions like:

   • What do you think of me?

   • What do you want to tell me today?

   • Is there anything you want to show/teach me?

3. **Lies block our ability to engage.** If you are not hearing, seeing, or sensing God, then please remember that your soul must be believing a lie and that lie is blocking your ability to connect. You are already ONE with Yahweh and God is not holding Himself back from you. So if you are

having trouble connecting, it is a simple fix and definitely is not Jesus withholding from you. At first, you may only get a glimpse or hear a word. That is ok and common. Your soul can focus and connect with Jesus in the spiritual realm, but it is also like a muscle that needs exercising. Your soul will need to practice focusing on Jesus and the spiritual realm to grow its capacity to stay connected longer. You are invited to LIVE from a constant connection with Jesus, which is also known as abiding. It takes time to mature there, but it is available to you if you choose it. Below, I have a whole section of tips for removing blocks and lies to help you connect better. But even then, your soul will still need practice and need to grow its capacity to stay consciously abiding in and connected to Jesus.

4.   **Forgive God if you are angry or offended with Him before choosing to engage.** Offense and accusations against God harden your soul from hearing God clearly (or even at all). You most likely won't be able to see or hear in an encounter because of the anger in your heart towards God. Instead, choose to forgive Jesus for the offense you have towards Him. The enemy has lied to you and you are hardening yourself against the Healer. Once you surrender the accusation and offense, then you can go to Him with the pain and receive healing and peace. To be clear, Jesus doesn't sin or do anything wrong, but that doesn't prevent our souls from being offended at God for something we perceived in our pain. Often, we are stuck (blocked) in accusations against God, for example, "Why did You allow _____" or "Where were You when _____" or "How can You be good or love if _____". Accusations, anger, and offense towards God ONLY hurt YOU. They keep you from Healing and Truth by your own choice. So, I challenge you to choose to forgive God so you can be healed and made whole.

5.   **Surrender the questions you want to be answered by God so they aren't an idol in your heart when you go on an encounter.** This is a big one. We WANT answers, especially

when we are in pain. It makes us feel in control. But answers are not what you need. Answers won't take away the pain you feel. You need Jesus, not answers, and He knows that. If you hold onto a question that you demand (or beg) be answered, then you are at risk of tainting an encounter with Jesus, if you can connect at all.

6. **It's best to not have an agenda when going on an encounter.** The Lord WANTS to heal you, He KNOWS exactly what's wrong, and His timing is always PERFECT. With that being said, when we go to God, He sometimes may choose to talk about different part of our heart than what we were seeking healing for. And that's ok! Trust His timing. If we have an agenda, we can miss what God really wants to do. Often, we need to grow our capacity to trust God before Jesus can address the BIG painful events and lies.

7. **Remember that you usually go on encounters through the lens or filters of your soul.** Your soul contains your free will so it is the one who calls the shots. You may encounter things that are not factual in the eyes of your soul because you experience the world(s) around you through the filters of your beliefs. The same way everything would be colored if you wore purple glasses—what you "see" is colored through the beliefs of your soul. Because of this, it's important to know the Bible and what it says about us and God so that you can discern what's true and not.

> 1 John 4:1 (BSB) "Beloved, do not believe every spirit, but test the spirits to see whether they are from God. For many false prophets have gone out into the world."

God is the same yesterday, today, and forever. He will not contradict Himself. So, if you encounter something that contradicts God or the Bible, you are encountering a lie in your soul! For example, if you see a vision of God being silent and distant with His arms crossed at you, is that the character of God described in the Bible? NO. But is that what you will see? Most likely you will because that is what you believe about Him. What you believe is how you will perceive the world around you. So, if you ever have an encounter experience that doesn't line up with the Bible or Truth, then call it out for what it is—a lie!

To remove a lie from filtering your encounter, it can be as easy as verbally saying something like "I break agreement with the lie that (insert the lie or call out what is anti-Biblical in your encounter)". I suggest you say it out loud because it audibly emphasizes your breaking agreement with the lie and its filtering effects. When you renounce the lie(s), usually the picture instantly changes because you removed the purple sunglasses. (More tips on trouble-shooting encounters are in the next section.)

8. **Go on encounters ONLY with God (Jesus, Father God, or Holy Spirit).** It is easy to get misled in the spirit world, so make sure you are always consciously and intentionally with someone in the Godhead. This is important when talking with other beings, whether it be the cloud of witnesses, angels, or especially a loved one who has passed. Our religious ideas will constantly be challenged in good ways when going on adventures with Yahweh. That is good, wonderful, and part of the process of transformation. BUT Satan will try to deceive you, and that is what I want you to be warned and on guard against.

> *2 Corinthians 11:14-15 (BSB) "Satan himself masquerades as an angel of light. It is not surprising, then, if his servants masqueraded as servants of righteousness."*

> *1 John 4:1 (BSB) "Beloved, do not believe every spirit, but test the spirits to see whether they are from God. For many false prophets have gone out into the world."*

9. **Be consistent with "repeat" triggers and hurts.** Think of it this way: our soul has a bad habit of carrying around pain. As much as it doesn't make sense, it is a HABIT even though it hurts us. Sometimes in healing, Jesus heals the pain, lie, AND habit. It is a one-and-done deal. Those healings are wonderful, and we appreciate it when it happens this way. BUT there is another manner of healing that is equally, possibly even more, precious; healing the moment to moment. Sometimes Jesus heals the hurts as we bring them to Him, but the habit of carrying the pain (or lie) remains. In this case, our healing WAS real and DID work the first time. But after our healing encounter, UNCONSCIOUSLY our soul acted out of its old habit and picked up the pain and lie again. Every habit CAN be changed, but it takes time and consistency. If your soul picks up the pain or lie again, bring it to Jesus again and again if you have to. It's simple: if we don't quit, our soul's bad habits WILL change. Better yet, the NEW habit will be bringing everything that hurts to Jesus! And THAT is possibly why this method of healing is more precious. Getting an instant healing is wonderful, but a new habit was not established. Receiving healing in the moment to moment is wonderful because our soul finds out that Jesus is patient, kind, and big enough for every hurt AND our soul created a new habit of going to Jesus for each pain it feels.

I know this was a lot of bullet points to keep in mind. Don't get overwhelmed or think you have to "figure it all out". These are tips and tools to help you begin engaging with Yahweh. It's a process and JOURNEY of transformation. These are just tips and things I've learned that can help you out.

Chapter Six:

TROUBLE-SHOOTING GETTING STUCK

Sometimes our soul freezes up and gets stuck when going on an encounter. Trauma and pain have a way of shutting down the soul because it is overwhelmed (and usually feels powerless or hopeless for a breakthrough). Many factors can cause a blockage or interference when we are encountering God. Remember that the spiritual realm is a whole new world, so it will take time and practice navigating a new place. In the spiritual realm, there isn't a rush to learn something "in time" because the spiritual realm is outside of the dimension of time. We are on a journey with Yahweh, joined in a beautiful love dance. He's not in a hurry. While everyone has their own journey of transformation, I hope this chapter helps bring clarity to this new world. Below is a list of common blocks that people face when trying to engage Jesus and the spiritual realm.

1. **Don't partner with discouragement or frustration.** Healing takes time and the enemy will do their best to lure you into an agreement with discouragement or frustration. Discouragement and frustration are from hell and are the enemy. Period. They always have and always will bring death and they SLOW your healing journey. Jesus is not discouraged or frustrated. This means you can choose not to partner with them.

   This life is a process and an eternal journey. There is not a "destination" or "arrival" that you achieve. Think of it as getting to dance with Jesus. How silly would it be to ask

Jesus, "Just tell me where I am standing at the end of the dance so I can go stand there now." You would have missed the beauty and connection found in dancing together! You literally ARE part of an eternal love dance, and the enjoyable part of the dance IS the dance, not trying to "arrive" at a certain spot spiritually that you made up in your head. Often lies have many layers that manifest in different ways in life. Don't be discouraged if a fear or another negative emotion is triggered after going on a healing encounter. Take the issue to Jesus again...and again if you have to. The heart can only handle so much surgery at one time, so healing happens in stages. Sometimes God comes in and heals an area of our soul in a moment, but more often than not, inner healing takes time and determination. And both types of healing are beautiful! If you receive an instant healing in your soul, you do not learn HOW to be whole so you'll be right back in pain and dysfunction within a matter of time if you don't know how to stay whole. This is why it is precious to walk through pain and healing WITH Jesus because you learn the tools and understanding so you don't fall back into dysfunction! It's beautiful to walk with Jesus because it builds history and connection with God as we work through our brokenness with Him.

2. **What to do with lies your soul believes.** There are different ways to call out lies that your soul believes. Below is ONE of many ways to do it. These 4 R's are a quick and easy way to combat lies in the soul. THIS IS NOT A FORMULA! God usually doesn't do the same thing twice, so it will always look different! He can skip steps or go out of order but this is a good base for addressing a lie during an encounter. When you realize you are believing a lie, you can:

   o Reveal!

      > Ask Jesus: "*What lie am I believing? What do YOU say about this lie?*"

○ Repent!

> Repent does not mean apologize! Repent means to make a U-turn. You are changing directions in the way you think. The goal is to acknowledge that the lie IS a lie, and then choose Jesus instead. It can look something like: "*I repent for believing the lie that (insert lie). It is a lie and it is the enemy. I choose not to agree with it anymore!*"

○ Replace!

> This is a critical step! You must replace the lie with truth from Jesus, or you won't have anything to combat the lie with. You can say something like: "*Jesus, I choose to give you this lie and not partner with it. I choose to believe what you say instead. So, Jesus, what is the truth to combat this lie? What do you say about it?*"

○ Rejoice!

> When Jesus tells you or gives you something. Thank Him for it! Be intentional to purposefully receive what Jesus tells you or gives you. Acknowledge the truth and allow it to become part of your belief system.

A quick note about lies: Don't lose heart when the enemy tells you that it's too hard or that it won't work. That is a lie! Your soul FEELS like that lie was the truth. Lies that we have believed for a long time feel like they are a part of us. Is that true? No. Lies are a leech on your soul, not part of it. But does it FEEL true? Yes. The question isn't "Is Jesus big enough?" The question is: will YOU choose to believe Jesus' truth and His freedom, or keep the comfortable but painful lies that are familiar?

3. **Walls are harmful—not helpful.** When we experience lots of pain or trauma, our soul will put up walls to protect itself. The problem is that walls actually trap the pain IN and keep

the healing OUT! They are a blockage in our soul. Walls hold us back from healing because we shut God out of our hearts too. We then become MORE hurt because we feel rejected by God, even though we were the ones to put the walls up to begin with! So, in our pain, we CHOOSE to entrap ourselves with the pain AND keep the healing out. All that to say, if you sense, see, or feel a wall in your soul AND you are ready to take that wall down, here are some things you can do:

o   Break AGREEMENT with that wall.

>   Your soul must decide it's ready to take down the wall. Jesus will not go against our free will. He is at the door (or wall) knocking. (Notice the verse didn't say "He's kicking the door down".) Once you decide you are ready to take the wall down, it's helpful to verbally say something like, "Soul, we acknowledge and decide that this wall is not helpful. It is a trap for us. So right now, I choose to no longer partner with this wall."

o   Ask Jesus (or Holy Spirit or Yahweh) how to take the wall down.

>   To take down the wall, They may:

- Tell you to speak something to the wall

- Give you a tool to use

- Tell you to do a prophetic act in the physical

- Or they may offer to take the wall down for you

There is an infinite list of ways God can tell you to take the wall down, so just do whatever He says. Take note of how things change with the wall gone. If parts of the wall remain, ask "Is there anyone I need to forgive or a lie I need freedom from?" Once your wall is gone, don't forget to thank Father for your latest breakthrough!

Everything the enemy does is a counterfeit of Truth. The enemy's walls of self-protection hurt us and bring death, BUT there is a kingdom version of walls. His name is Yahweh! Yes, seriously, the Lord IS our protection and our wall.

> Nahum 1:7 (BSB) "The LORD is good, a stronghold in the day of distress; He cares for those who trust in Him."

> Psalm 32:7 (BSB) "You are my hiding place. You protect me from trouble; You surround me with songs of deliverance."

> Psalm 46:1 (NLT) "God is our refuge and strength, always ready to help in times of trouble."

> Isaiah 43:2 (NLT) "When you go through deep waters, I will be with you. When you go through rivers of difficulty, you will not drown. When you walk through the fire of oppression, you will not be burned up; the flames will not consume you."

> Proverbs 18:10 (NLT) "The name of the Lord is a strong tower; the godly run to it and are safe."

I would encourage you to spend time with Yahweh and ask Him about His protection. What does it look like and mean for Him to be our refuge and hiding place? How are we hidden in Him? Remember, play 20 questions. The more truth you hear about being hidden in Him, the easier it will be for your soul to not put another wall up in the future. But sometimes the soul does anyways, just like that bad habit. Be consistent with taking the walls down again and again if you need to and the soul will learn over time that it doesn't need to self-protect.

4. **Talk with whoever you connect with best in the Godhead if you get stuck.** We all have different life experiences. Some of us have mom or dad wounds. Others have been deeply hurt by friends or siblings. Our life experiences affect our opinions and views of God: Yahweh, Jesus, and Holy Spirit. Our human heart doesn't have a grid for GOD in his

infinite vastness. So, we process the idea of GOD through our world experiences. We will expect God to treat us the same as our father, mother, and siblings/closest friends treated us. For example, if your earthly father was distant and cold, then you will subconsciously assume Yahweh will treat you the same. In the same way, our relationship with our mom usually translates over to our perception of Holy Spirit because they share the nurturer, teacher, and comforter roles. And according to scripture, Jesus is our brother and closest friend. So naturally, how our siblings or closest friends treated us is what we will expect Jesus to be like. This is why sometimes we will have a harder time connecting to different parts of the Godhead even though they are all one. So, if you are having a hard time in an encounter and get stuck, you can try talking to whoever your soul feels safest with in the Godhead and see if that helps you get past the block.

5. **Visit a familiar place when you get stuck.** You can revisit places and visions that you have had in encounters with Jesus. This is helpful if you get stuck in an encounter. If our soul shuts down, a helpful tool is to visit a familiar or favorite place in the spiritual realm that you have been before. Sometimes our soul needs to go to a safe place and reconnect with Yahweh there before moving forward.

    o   You can step away from the pain and reconnect in a different vision. There you can ask Jesus why you shut down. Again play 20 questions until you feel the courage to bring that painful area to Jesus for healing.

    o   OR another option would be for you to reconnect with Jesus in a different vision and choose to not go back to the trigger until another time. If your soul isn't ready to address a wound, trying to force your soul into it won't be helpful.

6. **The WONDERFUL backdoor of the obedience tool.** When we come up against a block that we just don't know how to

deal with, we can try the "obedience tool"! It's probably my favorite strategy and is super helpful. All you have to do is ask something like "Jesus, how do I get rid of this thing in my life?" Then DO whatever Jesus says to do! That's it! He is GOD and when He speaks something—it is FINAL.

For example, Jesus once told a friend to "tear up a piece of paper and this thing will be gone". Usually physically tearing up a piece of paper would have NO effect on the spiritual realm and soul wounds. BUT because Jesus said it would, now there was a decree in place! Demons are subject to spiritual law, so in this case, when my friend tore up the piece of paper, the demons HAD to obey because she was in line with a decree from Jesus. There was no arguing. The demon was PISSED but left instantly and painlessly. What a relief! That was a true story from the first time I learned about the obedience tool. Since then, I have used this tool over and over again. Sometimes Jesus tells us to do odd things in the physical realm and sometimes He has us do things in an encounter. Either way, Jesus is faithful and ALWAYS has a solution and what we need.

7. **If none of these troubleshooting tools helped, DON'T GIVE UP.** I understand deep pain and trying to navigate through trauma. I have been there many times and am speaking from my personal experience—don't give up. I knew and understood these tools when I had a full psychiatric breakdown and these tools didn't help me. In my youth, I zealously picked a fight with a large prince (demon bad guy). I was out of bounds spiritually and also had a poor understanding of my identity and spiritual laws. I was all zeal and no wisdom. I got my butt kicked—bad. That is what caused the full breakdown. I couldn't function...just brushing my hair was SO stressful to me that it brought me to tears. I tried so hard to connect with Jesus in the middle of it, but there was nothing my soul could feel. I knew that my spirit was one with Jesus. I knew I wasn't alone and that Jesus WAS indeed talking to me. I was just too broken to hear Him. In that moment, I could have gotten offended at Him. I

could have held an accusation against Jesus and would have felt justified in it because He could have revealed Himself to me. But I intentionally chose not to.

Even in the worst of my breakdown, I knew I was still one with Jesus. I knew He was the only Healer, and I knew that choosing to be offended against Him would only HURT me more. I didn't understand, but I chose not to demand or even focus on the questions I had. Instead, I choose to focus on Jesus. I felt nothing. I didn't see visions. I couldn't hear Jesus at all. I couldn't even visit my favorite places in the spiritual realm. BUT I chose to set my intention towards Jesus. In the silence and darkness I felt in my soul, I focused on Him. I used my free will to turn to Jesus even though I felt nothing in return. The key was that I didn't give up. I persevered in the face of the enemy's accusations against Jesus for "not showing up in my darkest moment". And over time, my soul healed. I knew my ability to connect was a SOUL issue, not Jesus abandoning me when I was hurting. I knew I was already one with Him, so my lack of feelings was a SYMPTOM of a very broken soul. I was patient and intentional. Jesus was big enough to heal EVERY part that was broken from my zealousness. I meditated on truth and worshiped until my soul was ready to connect again and come out of the darkness.

Meditation and encounters go hand-in-hand with this journey. You can lose or forget what happens when you engage with Yahweh, especially at the beginning while your soul is learning to navigate this whole new world. You can think of it like a really cool dream that you don't think you'll ever forget...then you forget. Unless you write it down, tell it over and over, or think about it often, our souls simply forget and go back to the pain that they are familiar with. You can forget even the greatest miracles when you are lost and blind in pain. Meditation is key to reminding your soul and training a NEW way of thinking and living. Encounters give you the personal and intimate keys you need for your circumstances, but they can be easily forgotten. Stand on the Word of the Lord. Meditate on the Word and engage with the living Word as often as you can. Eventually, you learn to LIVE out of that connection and encounter with Yahweh, and I cover that more at the end of the book.

All of this chapter comes from 14 years of my own personal journey. I was broken, blind, offended, and lost...religion didn't help me out of any of my pain. I believed in Jesus as my savior, but my soul was buried in pain and torment. Even though my spirit was one with Jesus, I didn't know what had happened and my soul remained in torment. My only comfort was the head knowledge that I have collected over the years, but it acted like a tease and frustration instead of bringing me to freedom. Everything changed when I began to have a personal relationship with Jesus. Head knowledge turned into heart revelation and soul freedom. Jesus spoke to ME, personally. Jesus loved ME. Jesus healed ME. As I have grown, my healing and breakthrough has accelerated because I trust Jesus at deeper levels. Your journey is your own. It will look different than mine, but I can guarantee it will take time and patience.

This book, but especially this chapter is a firehose of information. It will take time to digest and absorb the information and tools in this chapter. When all you have ever known is the dimension your body lives in, it is scary and challenging to discover a whole new realm to live in and from. You have started an eternal journey. There is no "destination" or "arrival" point in eternity, so enjoy the love dance with Jesus. I invite you to start today. Invite Jesus into your mess and pain exactly how it is. He's got the answers and wisdom and healing you need. He's knocking, will you let Him in?

> Revelation 3:20 "Behold I stand at the door and knock, anyone who hears my voice AND opens the door. I will come in and have deep and blissful intimacy with him and he with me." [Author translation]

Chapter Seven:

GROWING UP

We have a beautiful invitation before us to grow up. Religion has created a system that produces needy and immature Christians that sit around and wait to die so they can escape to Heaven. I grew up in religion thinking that this time on earth was only to win souls and bide our time until we die, or until Jesus came back. Immature Christianity was never God's plan for His kids. He desires for us to be mature sons of God who can be entrusted with ruling and reigning just like HE would. Every believer starts out as a baby after being born again. This is the order of things, and Yahweh, our Father, cherishes us in our infancy just like a new parent adores their baby. However, no parent desires or hopes for their child to STAY a baby forever. Yahweh invites us to govern and rule and reign with Him. He is excited to see His kids grow up to be powerful sons of God that change the universe for the better. Immaturity holds us back from the fullness that God has for us. And for some, it is a great deception because they are ignorantly immature while thinking they are "great Christians".

> *1 Corinthians 3:1 (AMP) "I could not talk to you as to spiritual people, but [only] as to worldly people [dominated by human nature], mere infants [in the new life] in Christ!"*
>
> *1 Corinthians 14:20 (AMP) "...do not be children [immature, childlike] in your thinking; be infants in [matters of] evil [completely innocent and inexperienced], but in your minds be mature [adults]."*

Galatians 4:3 (ESV) "In the same way we also, when we were children, were enslaved to the elementary principles of the world."

Ephesians 4:14 (ESV) "so that we may no longer be children, tossed to and fro by the waves and carried about by every wind of doctrine, by human cunning, by craftiness in deceitful schemes."

Hebrews 5:12 (BSB) "Although by this time you ought to be teachers, you need someone to reteach you the basic principles of God's word. You need milk, not solid food!"

Paul addresses the immaturity of believers many times, it's not a new thing. ALL of us start out immature in the beginning. ALL of us start out as babies when we are born again...the intention was that we would grow up though! We were intended to RULE and REIGN with Christ. Babies who are still fleshly are not powerful and ready to reign with Jesus. There is so much more for us, and it is already in us because of Jesus! Choosing to mature requires us to take responsibility and lean into the stretching that maturing brings.

Ephesians 1:4-5 (NLT) "Even before he made the world, God loved us and chose us in Christ to be holy and without fault in his eyes. God decided in advance to adopt us into his own family by bringing us to himself through Jesus Christ. This is what he wanted to do, and it gave him great pleasure." [Emphasis mine]

The word "adopt" in the original language is not the same as our perception of the word today. When we hear "adopt", we think of an orphan who was taken in (adopted) by a new family. As beautiful as this sounds that God "adopted" us, this passage means something so much better! In the Jewish culture, adoption is the POWERFUL moment that a father presents his son to the tribe as a MATURE son that can do business in his name, as the father himself! WOW! A son is fully the son of the father from his birth, but when he matures, he is "adopted" and has the authority and trust of the father!

In the Jewish culture, adoption is something the son chooses to grow into. A son comes from his father and is like him because the son is made from his father. (Remember, we were made in the image of God himself! We are His offspring from the beginning too!) Then, in the Jewish culture, when a son is of age, he receives a bar mitzvah. This is the celebration of the son transitioning from a child to a man. From that point on, the son is treated and expected to act like a man. No one grows up overnight though, there is still lots for the son to learn and grow in before he is considered mature. Maturing is a process, a journey, and can't be cut short. Mistakes will be made, pride gets ironed out, and rash zeal turns to consistent wisdom. As the son matures, the father disciples his son's character and mentors him in the family business. Then, once the son can be trusted to handle business just like the father would, once the son has matured and can make powerful decisions, then the father will "ADOPT" him. The father will call together the elders of the town and gather the family. Then, in front of everyone, the father will publicly ADOPT his son. From that point on, the family and tribe know that the son has the authority to act and do business in the name of the father, as the father himself. This is maturity.

Before He made the world, before we sinned, God's plan was for us to be part of the family. But the intention wasn't for us to be the eternal little kids of the family. The original design was for us to mature so that we can rule and reign as Yahweh does, in His name and as Him. We were made in the very image of God so that we can be like Him...not just in looks but in maturity and action. Will we ever become Creator God, King of Kings, Yahweh himself? No, obviously not. But we ARE kings. He's just the KING of kings. We are priests. He is the HIGH priest. He will always outrank us, which is rightfully so. The invitation is for us to step into our identities and be His hands and voice on the earth.

So HOW do we mature?

- **Act like Jesus.** Yes, act like Him until you ARE like Him. The more you act like Jesus, the faster you become more like Jesus in action and thought! How does a child mature? A child watches daddy wash the car and tries to help. Does he actually help? No. And it takes three times longer anytime you have a child "help". But when they help, they learn, little by little, how to do things. Over time, they are actually helping wash the car and then grow to be able to wash it on their own! So act like Jesus, and you'll become like Him along the way.

- **Go to Jesus as the source for everything in life.** The religious institution has people dependent on the pastor for their spiritual "feedings" and direction, and they often expect him to do all the work—for their healing and in the community.

> *1 John 2:27 (NLT) "You have received the Holy Spirit, and he lives within you, so you don't need anyone to teach you what is true. For the Spirit teaches you everything you need to know, and what he teaches is true—it is not a lie. So just as he has taught you, remain in fellowship with Christ." [Emphasis mine]*

We don't NEED a teacher; we have THE Teacher of Teachers IN us! Go to the Source. As we allow Jesus to be our Source, we will not walk around as dependents on a system, but we will become nation shakers— a bridge from Heaven to this earth. Part of maturing is to stop sucking from the bottle of the institution and instead be filled in our soul by the reality our spirit already lives in. An important note on this, we are all part of the body of Christ and we are called to bear one another's burdens.

Occasionally needing help from fellow believers is absolutely ok. This life is hard, and when we are hit with trauma, it can be hard to connect with Yahweh and sort through the pain. So, to be clear, needing help to get through a season is very different from a constant dependency on someone to be our source.

- **Learn from your mistakes.** Children who are learning to walk, do not start out walking perfectly. It is understood that a child won't walk or ride a bike perfectly the first time. The same level of patience and grace needs to be given to ourselves as we grow spiritually. We are learning to walk in Christ and won't walk perfectly at first. We will fall and bump our knees, but we have a loving Father cheering us and helping us back up. Father is patient. He knows we are learning and going to make mistakes. When we make a mistake, the solution is simple…bring it to Jesus! Ask Him what happened and what your soul was believing when you made the mistake. Bring it to Jesus. If you do this, then everything becomes an opportunity to GROW you! You learn more from failure and mistakes than you learn when you do something correctly. In the same way, you grow more in hard times than you do in easy times. So, it becomes a win-win! You can't lose! You either do it well or learn from it and do it better next time!

- **Stay humble.** The moment we think we know everything—is the moment we stop growing. If we want to continually grow and mature, then we must not become prideful or offended. There is an infinite amount of knowledge in Yahweh. Do you really think our pea brains are a match for the endless majesty and wisdom in Yahweh? I didn't think so. So, stay humble in all you do, that way you won't be stunted in growth in any part of your soul.

- **Be self-aware.** How is your thought life? Do your actions look like Jesus? Why do you do what you do? As we begin to pay attention to our thoughts, actions, and habits, we are taking the first step towards maturing and transformation.

To be clear, ALL of this process requires faith. From the moment you chose Jesus, you used faith. We use faith to have a personal relationship with God, and in faith, we test everything against the Word of God. Likewise, we ALL started out deceived, and we are ALL on a journey out of that deception. Every lie we break off and every hurt that gets healed helps us walk more in Truth and less in the lies that we were deceived by. This is just part of the journey of transformation. For fear of being deceived, a lot of people choose to not grow up and engage with Yahweh. They don't want to "get weird" or "be deceived", so instead they stay deceived in the box that they created. We are all in the beautiful and messy process of sonship whether we recognize it or not.

Lastly, Jesus is not impatiently waiting for us to "get a grip" and grow up. However, He is looking for the believers who will give their undying "YES!" to Him. Jesus releases us to be fully free to make choices WITHOUT CONDEMNATION while at the same time inviting us to join Him in the eternal love dance. Jesus wants the will of the Father to be done on the earth so death and sickness will have their end. But He won't do this at the cost of taking away our free will. Instead, Jesus is waiting for us to join Him on the cross, die to the flesh, and be raised up as Him and in Him. He is waiting for us to submit our perfectly free will, under the will of Yahweh so we can be adopted as mature sons. When we choose this, nothing is more powerful in all of the universe.

Chapter Eight:

THE MYSTERIOUS AND WONDERFUL

This eternal journey we are on is the most wonderful adventure of all! It is a wild ride that continues to challenge the box that I had myself or Jesus in. The heights and depths and realms and dimensions are endless, just like His love. Yahweh is infinite, all-powerful, and over-flowing in majesty—beyond any word's description and any mind's comprehension. Yahweh is so marvelous that He HAS to scale Himself down for us to even begin to comprehend and engage with Him. For example, when Jesus scales Himself down to King of Kings in an encounter, your face will be on the ground and you still aren't low enough. Then Jesus can choose to scale Himself more and show up to you as a friend that you can see face to face. There is so much more than we could possibly think or imagine—He is infinite in His wonder. It is scary and exciting and wonderful and strange all rolled into one. Even the unusual and scary parts are filled with the wonder and goodness of Yahweh.

This book is a firehose of information. I also didn't fully explain every concept and I intentionally left questions unanswered. The purpose of this book is to point you to Jesus and I hope you bring every drop of this firehose to Jesus. Every concept and unanswered question can be a springboard in your trust and friendship with Jesus. All you need is Him and I want to help you see that and grow in Him. If I were to give you some advice in this eternal journey, it would be these few things:

1. Stay close to Jesus

   > He is everything. He is the Source, Life, Healing, Provision, EVERYTHING. Being close to Him is what matters most. Concerns of this world are momentary, but what we do and build with Jesus is eternal. Be conscious of Him in all things...from doing the dishes, to relationships, to bills, to the future. Bring Him consciously and intentionally into everything you do. Not only will your life transform, but it will change the world around you.

2. Stay humble and flexible

   > I know I mentioned this in the last chapter, but it really is vitally important. Don't get stunted by thinking you know or understand something. Even within the attributes of God, there are layers. For example, you can eternally learn more about the goodness of God. He is infinite. So, stay humble in all things... even children and the ants have so much they can teach you.

3. Persevere, do not give up.

   > Jesus is faithful in the midst of a fleeting world. He is the only thing we can count on and trust. Circumstances change, people act human, and trouble is guaranteed in this life. In an uncertain world, only ONE thing is certain. And His name is Jesus. When all hell has broken loose— He is still Provider, Healer, and King of Kings. Jesus is big enough to carry us through everything we face. So, I challenge you to persevere and do not give up. Trust Jesus in all ways and at all costs.

   Jeremiah 32:27 (ESV) "Behold, I am the LORD, the God of all flesh. Is anything too hard for me?"

4. Choose Jesus no matter the pain, confusion, or circumstance.

   > When pain comes, the enemy accuses Yahweh of the brokenness that Satan caused. The greater the pain, the

greater the accusation the enemy pushes. It can be so difficult to choose Jesus in the midst of great pain and unanswered questions. But please, do NOT agree with the enemy (who hates you and is trying to destroy your life). Jesus is good and He is the only healer. There is no other way out of pain except in Him. If you harden yourself against Yahweh because of pain and questions, you sever your ability to be healed and whole. So, in all things, choose Jesus. Bill Johnson says "To have peace that surpasses your understanding, you must give up your right to understand." Choose Jesus over the pain and unanswered questions and you will have peace that surpasses understanding and healing to your soul.

As you practice these things and grow your soul's capacity to focus on and engage with the spiritual realm, you can learn to operate in BOTH worlds at once. Instead of needing a quiet place, you can practice connecting with Jesus while going about your everyday life. THIS is abiding. It will take time to get there. At first, you have to teach the soul to focus and engage with the spiritual world. But as you mature in this, you will begin to more easily focus on the spiritual, while also being able to focus on and operate in the physical. You can grow to become FULLY conscious and engaged with both places simultaneously. You are a multi-dimensional being that can also live with a multi-dimensional consciousness.

I spent a lot of time in this book explaining soul wounds and how to get unstuck, but that is just the beginning. Engaging with Yahweh (going on encounters) won't always be about you and your soul wounds. Dealing with the soul wounds is simply a pre-requisite before we can ascend. Those soul blocks have to be removed so you can go on adventures and missions with Yahweh. He wants to teach you how to fly, and He will…but first, you must heal. Then you can ascend!

I am upfront and clear that I don't know or understand everything. In fact, the more I learn, the more I see just HOW little I know and understand. Part of me feels like a kindergartener trying to write a book on quantum physics. I know so little, and yet it has been on my heart to write and point people to Yahweh. He's just the best in every way and I want to help people find Him and reject religion in every form.

> 1 Corinthians 13:12-13 (NLT) "Now we see things imperfectly, like puzzling reflections in a mirror, but then we will see everything with perfect clarity. All that I know now is partial and incomplete, but then I will know everything completely, just as God now knows me completely. Three things will last forever—faith, hope, and love—the greatest of these is love."

> 1 Corinthians 13:9 (NLT) "Now our knowledge is partial and incomplete, and even the gift of prophecy reveals only part of the whole picture."

Even Paul didn't claim to know it all, but he shared what he knew and changed the world because of it. Even if I were to know everything, which I don't, many things are beyond explanation. Spiritual concepts and depths are too much for our pea brains to handle, and it's designed to be that way. We are pea-brained leading the pea-brained. When you see the reality of our pea-brained state of being, it really takes the pressure off of trying to figure it all out. So, let's go to the one who isn't pea-brained and enjoy the love dance you have joined in!

When I was a young mom, wife, and busy... I mean BUSY being a kid's pastor, I was wrestling with how much time to spend with God. This was before I learned about the tree of life and that "should" is a demon, but it still led me to a life-changing encounter with Yahweh. I asked Papa, "How much time should I spend with you each day? David Hogan spends 4 hours a day and Heidi Baker spends 6 hours each day in the secret place with you. If I am seated in eternity, then we have all of eternity together, right? How many hours (in my thinking—how many hours of lost sleep) should I be spending with You a day?"

Yahweh laughed at me and said, "Oh? You don't think you'll be busy in eternity?" I was just about to defend myself when Yahweh showed me this incredible picture of Heaven. It was like a flawless bee hive filled with glory, boundless joy, utter peace, and in perfect rhythm. There was SO much to do, so many missions and adventures and realms to explore. (There were no people sitting on clouds playing harps!) Yahweh explained, "Even in eternity, there is busyness. There is no boredom here, and there are infinite things you can do. Even here, outside of time, rarely do people come away and seek Me in the secret place." Yahweh then pulled back the flesh veil on His heart to show me the most intimate secret places in His heart. There were less than a handful of people there with Him in that place. With all the beings in Heaven, it broke my heart to see so few taking the time to come away into the secret place. I knew the secret place was an invitation for all and there was no judgment against those who didn't choose it. Yahweh loves our gift of free will, and in Heaven, there is no "should" or condemnation. As I took in the reality that there will always be busyness even in eternity, Yahweh continued, "Jessica, the question is not how much time "should" you spend with me. The real question is how much of Me do you want?" Yahweh spread His arms open wide in an invitation, eyes of fire stirring the very core of my being. I was overwhelmed by the question and what I saw. I responded, "I want to be a junkie for Your Presence. I want to be the one to minister to Your Heart. I will come away to the secret place and stay with You there. I want all of You." Yahweh smiled and I was forever changed.

So, how much of Yahweh do you want? To gain His heart, we must give Him ours first. And to the extent we give Him our heart, is the same measure that Yahweh gives us His. He loved us first and offers us His heart first, but we have to choose Him and open the door to let Him in. There is no condemnation; you are truly free to choose how much and how deep you want to go. We are each on our personal and beautiful journey with

Jesus. It's a wild, weird, and wonderful adventure that we are invited into and decide how much of it we want.

I hope this book and series encourage you in your journey with Yahweh. It's not easy, but it is the most wonderful thing in all of the universe. The beginning is the hardest so don't give up. Jesus is trustworthy, faithful, and big enough. One final tip, the quicker and deeper we surrender, the quicker and fuller the breakthrough we will see. I would say be blessed, but you already ARE blessed! So instead, I will say in closing, "The best is yet to come. Happy dancing."

RESOURCES FOR THE JOURNEY AHEAD

Books: hard copies are great, but a lot of these books are cheaper on kindle.

Sonship and undoing religion
- Divine Adoption - Jesudian Sylvester
- Swallowed up by life – Jesudian Sylvester
- Legacy of Sonship - Ricky Nieuwenhuis
- The Shack- William Paul Young
- Treasures of Darkness III Part 1: Foundations of a Transcendent Life—Joseph Sturgeon

Inner Healing
- Emotional Healing in 3 Easy Steps - Praying Medic
- Heart Made Whole - Christa Black

Seeing in the Spirit
- Seeing in the Spirit Made Simple - Praying Medic

YouTube Videos: Search these titles on YouTube to find the videos.

- **Living from Heaven Chris Blackeby**
  This is profoundly freeing for anyone wanting to leave religion and understand identity better. This sermon I have listened to repeatedly more than any other sermon!
  https://www.youtube.com/h?v=LNxMVsqhQTO&list=PLpVBWlnJzRDlpHClQDWue1dBUmlyL3wB&index=2&t=1233s

- **Foundations by Jesudian Sylvester**
  It is a 10-part series on the foundations of the gospel. He is an EXCELLENT teacher and deconstructs religious gospel in full. I

highly recommend it to every believer!

https://www.youtube.com/st?list=PLjzPWhJn4GdUTzIsY3CEGGSO2bGFluNtk

• **Sonship, Identity, and Maturing**
Dan Mohler's- The truth, Faith, Deliverance
This sermon is a wonderful, compact teaching on the truth of the gospel and getting our hearts free from bondage!

https://www.youtube.com/
watch?v=LpVBWInJzRDBXwkvarHvhbiLrHBRXz93&inde=3

• **How to detox your brain Part 1 and Part 2**
Detoxing your mind with Caroline Leaf is a powerful teaching on the brain and understanding the need to renew the mind and how thoughts affect your physical brain. She teaches a more technical and scientific style which is helpful for a lot of people.

https://www.youtube.com/watch?v=Ea8pHeetkgo

• **Start in rest - Chris Blackeby**
This sermon is wonderful at breaking down what rest is and how to live in the REST that Jesus has for us.

https://www.youtube.com/watch?v=mST3qX9_
list=PLpVBWInJzRDIpHCIQDWue1dBUmlyL3wB&index=1&t=4016s

• **Sons live by the goodness of God Chris Blackeby**
This sermon helps shift our heart from orphans to sons!

https://www.youtube.com/watch?v=mxYjVBIL4oM

POEMS OF A LOVER OF JESUS

This section is simply a few of the poems/songs that I have written over the years. These are very close to my heart and very personal to me, yet I felt Yahweh asked if I would share them. So, I am reluctantly obeying. I trust that they will minister to you as they have to me.

The first poem was written while I was healing from my miscarriage. It is very personal to me, but I shared it in the hope it helps those who are grieving find Yahweh in their pain. I chose Him and am now whole because of Him. You can be whole in your body and heart even after a great tragedy. He is our great comforter and our healer. May those who have lost, be whole again.

Broken to Whole

In the midst of the heartbreak
In the midst of all the wrong
I look to you Jesus
My strength, my healer

I'm longing for my baby
The pain feels too great to bear
But I look to you Jesus
My strength, my healer

A million questions run through my mind
To torment my pain-filled heart
I choose to not get lost in it all

Instead, I look to you Jesus
My strength, my healer

When will the storm stop raging?
There's nothing I can do
So instead of pulling away
I look to you Jesus
My strength, my healer

I know you didn't want this
I know you didn't cause this
So, I choose you and cry with you
I look to you Jesus
My strength, my healer

You're the only one who can heal
You're the only one to calm the storm
You're the only way out of my great despair

So I give it all to you

I give you my pain
I give you my baby

I look to you Jesus
My strength, my healer

The Song of the Ravished Lover

My beloved is calling me
My soul comes alive
I hear the whisper of Love calling me

He's calling from the wilderness
Saying will you come?
The cost is everything
Will you still come?

And I cry yes, my undying yes!
All I am is yours
I'm no longer my own

The secret place beckons me come
You've called me your friend
You've called me your lover

Fully bonded, fully submitted
Through my fears and past my walls
Whatever the cost

I come and I'm undone
The wilderness is not a wilderness
I've been met by Love

I'm captivated
I'm lost in His gaze
All else fades

I joined the eternal love dance
Lost in eternal bliss
I've been won by Love

I Choose You

In spite of my feelings
In spite of my questions
Still, I choose you

In times of abundance
In times of devastation
Still, I choose you

Even when pain blames you
Even when I can't see
Still, I choose you

In sickness and in health
For richer or for poorer
I will still choose you

Where else could I go?
Only you have the words of life
There is no one like you

Where else could I go?
Only you are the healer
The only redeemer

So I lay it all down
I give you my all
Let it be a burnt offering
Pain and all

I choose you
Again and again, I will choose you

I choose you
Because you first chose me

Color Outside the Lines

Take me to the edge of myself
I want to be undone

Make me uncomfortable
I want to know your heart
Captivate and overwhelm me
I just want you

Break up the ground
Tear down the walls
I'm ready for the mess
I want it all

Unthrottled, unbridled
Out of the box

Color outside the line
Color on me
Color on you
Color outside the line

SCRIPTURE PERMISSIONS

Scriptures are quoted from five main translations:

- Berean Study Bible (BSB)

- English Standard Version (ESV)

- New Living Translation (NLT)

- Amplified Bible (AMP)

- The Passion Translation (TPT)

Permissions are as follows:

ABOUT THE AUTHOR

Jessica was a nobody from nowhere, then she discovered she was a son of God! Through the years, she has been on a journey of discovering her identity and growing a personal friendship with Jesus...and now she helps others do the same!

Seraph Creative is a collective of artists, writers, theologians & illustrators who desire to see the body of Christ grow into full maturity, walking in their inheritance as Sons of God on the Earth.

Sign up to our newsletter to know about future exciting releases.

Visit our website :

www.seraphcreative.org

Made in the USA
Columbia, SC
26 July 2025

61032646R00052